The Decorated Journal

CREATING BEAUTIFULLY
EXPRESSIVE JOURNAL PAGES

Gwen Diehn

LARK BOOKS

A Division of Sterling Publishing Co., Inc.
New York

 *for* EDIE GREENE

Editor: Jane LaFerla
Illustrations: Gwen Diehn
Principal Photographer:
  Keith Wright, keithwright.com
Cover Designer: Barbara Zaretsky
Assistant Editor: Susan Keiffer
Associate Art Director: Shannon Yokeley
Editorial Assistance: Delores Gosnell
Intern: Megan S. McCarter
Supplementary Photography: Aleia Woolsey

The Library of Congress has cataloged the hardcover edition as follows:

Diehn, Gwen, 1943-
  The decorated journal : creating beautifully expressive journal pages /
Gwen Diehn.
    p. cm.
  Includes index.
  ISBN 1-57990-651-6
  1. Photograph albums. 2. Scrapbooks--Design. 3. Diaries. 4. Bookbinding.
  5. Artists' books. I. Title.
  TR465.D5297 2005
  745.593--dc22

                    2004028748

10 9 8 7 6 5 4 3

Published by Lark Books, A Division of
Sterling Publishing Co., Inc.
387 Park Avenue South, New York, N.Y. 10016

First Paperback Edition 2006
© 2005, Gwen Diehn

Distributed in Canada by Sterling Publishing,
c/o Canadian Manda Group, 165 Dufferin Street
Toronto, Ontario, Canada M6K 3H6

Distributed in the United Kingdom by GMC Distribution Services,
Castle Place, 166 High Street, Lewes, East Sussex, England BN7 1XU

Distributed in Australia by Capricorn Link (Australia) Pty Ltd.,
P.O. Box 704, Windsor, NSW 2756 Australia

The written instructions, photographs, designs, patterns, and projects in this
volume are intended for the personal use of the reader and may be repro-
duced for that purpose only. Any other use, especially commercial use, is
forbidden under law without written permission of the copyright holder.

Every effort has been made to ensure that all the information in this book is
accurate. However, due to differing conditions, tools, and individual skills,
the publisher cannot be responsible for any injuries, losses, and other
damages that may result from the use of the information in this book.

If you have questions or comments about this book, please contact:
Lark Books, 67 Broadway, Asheville, NC 28801, (828) 253-0467

Manufactured in China

ISBN 13: 978-1-57990-651-1 (hardcover) 978-1-57990-956-7 (paperback)
ISBN 10: 1-57990-651-6 (hardcover) 1-57990-956-6 (paperback)

For information about custom editions, special sales, premium and
corporate purchases, please contact Sterling Special Sales Department
at 800-805-5489 or specialsales@sterlingpub.com.

CONTENTS

Introduction

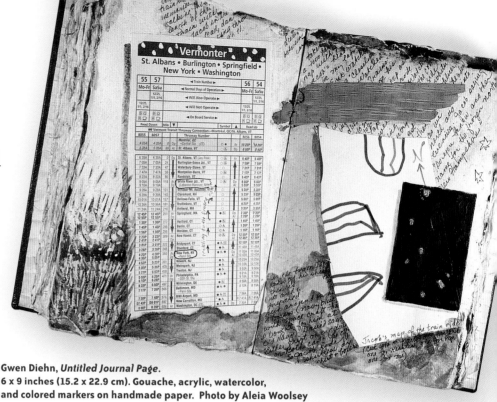

Gwen Diehn, *Untitled Journal Page*.
6 x 9 inches (15.2 x 22.9 cm). Gouache, acrylic, watercolor,
and colored markers on handmade paper. Photo by Aleia Woolsey.

While riding the train north from New York to New Hampshire in late December,
I passed the time by making a collage of a train time table, some birch bark,
and a map by Jacob Diehn.

hen Lark Books approached me about writing a follow-up to *The Decorated Page*, my first book on visual journaling, they were clear that they wanted a stand-alone book, one that would be as useful to those who had never seen *The Decorated Page* as it would be to those who had read it and reread it several times. The new book needed to have its own unique content as well as sufficient basic content to be accessible to newcomers.

I began to think about the recent books I had seen on journaling. I also began to pay close attention to the frequently asked questions that kept popping up on the several internet art journal lists to which I subscribe. At the same time, I had the good fortune to come across several old illustrated journals that looked nothing like the journals that dominate the scene today. In considering all these elements, I discovered how much more there was of the topic to investigate and ultimately share with you. As you work with your own text and images, I hope you'll find the information presented here to be helpful in creating expressive journal pages.

The first chapter of the book addresses one of the most persistent questions that I've encountered on internet lists and in classes and workshops I've taught—"What mate-rial did you use to get that color, texture, effect, etc.?" This question was the genesis of a materials section that takes the position that *less is more*, provided that the less is of top quality and that you understand how it works.

Because this section tells *how* materials work and inter-act, it can help you make more informed choices when buying adhesives, paints, papers, and other materials. You'll find information about color mixing, for example, that will equip you to mix your own colors from good quality paints.

The next section, How Does Your Journal See the World, relates the ways different people throughout his-tory and around the world have interpreted what they call reality by representing that world in images and text. While layered pages can be great fun and are very popu-lar today, they don't represent the only possibility for working with images as well as text in a journal. This sec-tion discusses many ideas for using your journal to explore as well as express different worldviews. It includes, among other ideas, a look at symbolic, natural-ist, and creative journal keeping, as well as some ideas for processes that are frequently used in these different kinds of journals.

The next major section, Pages in Stages, strips away the mystery behind pages that may look complicated and difficult. There are many different styles of page represented in this section, some very simple, others many-layered and complex. Once you see how they were done, you can easily try out your own combinations and approaches.

The last chapter of the book, The Reluctant Bookbinder, answers another one of the most persistent questions that I've encountered: "Where can I find a blank book that has [fill in your own exacting specifications as to paper type, size, shape, cover material, price, etc.]"?

In my experience, often the answer to this question is, sadly, "Nowhere, because there just aren't that many people who love to write on flattened-out lunch bags bound into a nice little soft-leather cover with a pocket added to the second-to-last section; so manufacturers can't afford to make them." But *you* can afford to make these wonderfully eccentric, perfect journals. The last chapter will not only tell you how, but will help you make your own journal (and not expire from the effort), even if you are definitely not interested in becoming a bookbinder. Being able to make your own journal will enable you to use the exact kind of paper(s) you love, have exactly the right size and shape of book, and even have special little touches that can never be found in purchased journals. Best of all, you will need no more sophisticated equipment than what you can find in the junk drawer in your kitchen.

Throughout this book, as in *The Decorated Page*, I've included short essays that introduce you to journal keepers and journal lore in order to build a context for the practice of keeping a journal. Reading about the widely varying uses that have been made of illustrated journals and the myriad contexts in which they have been created can jump start some explorations of your own. Personally, I was delighted to learn that Francis Galton considered keeping a journal right up there in importance with procuring a team of good strong camels to get himself and his expedition across a desert. I felt very close to Muriel Foster when I saw that she disregarded the lines in her fishing diary and painted a lovely scene of the stream in which she was fishing right across the middle of two pages. And I was positively enraptured by Jennifer Bartlett's ability to not only make the best of a bad situation when she painted and drew the same really rather pedestrian garden scene day after day for almost a whole rainy year, but to transform this base material into a spectacular body of work.

I think these examples from journaling luminaries will inspire you as they did me. They teach us all how to look and look again, and then look yet again. These journal keepers' patient looking and recording opens our eyes to the richness that is everywhere.

Gwen Diehn, *Untitled Journal Page*. 6 x 9 inches (15.2 x 22.9 cm). Watercolor, gouache, fluid acrylic, pen on handmade paper. Photo by Aleia Woolsey

Materials &
How to Use Them

he difficult truth about art materials is that the materials themselves are not as important as what you do with them. Another hard fact, which you already know, is that art is a practice, and as such it needs to be tended and nurtured by engaging in it on a regular basis. No product is going to make your journal or other artwork come alive and be inspired. Only you can do that by working and playing every day with your small supply of excellent materials.

Less is More:
On Selecting Materials

"Less is more," said architect Mies van der Rohe when explaining one of the basic principles underlying his spare and elegant work. And even before Mies, back in the 14th century, a philosopher named William of Occam insisted that, "What can be done with fewer is done in vain with more." These are good thoughts to keep in mind when buying art materials. "That may be,"

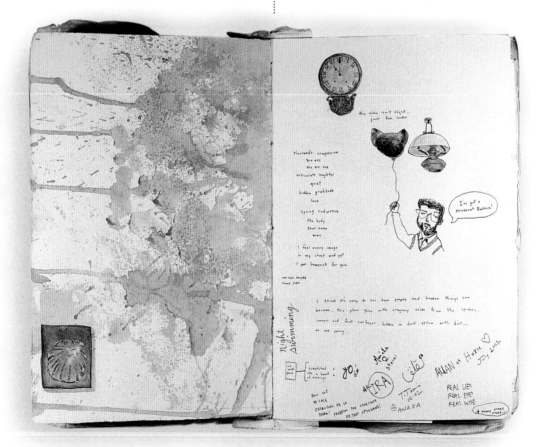

Ivy Smith, *Shell and Muskrat Balloon,* **2004. 11¹/₄ x 9 inches (28.6 x 22.9 cm).**
Bound Journal, ink, watercolor. Photo by Aleia Woolsey

Materials for journal keeping

you protest, "but if I can only find out what kind of paint was used to do the background of this page, my own work would take off and might look just as good." So off you go in search of the magic paint. But when you find it, you have to buy five jars because it only comes in sets labeled "Autumn Colors Collection" and "Spring Colors Collection." And, it's so thinly pigmented and filled with chalky stuff that you can't use it to mix anything, making it necessary for you to buy a separate bottle if you want a slightly more yellowish orange.

When the buying crazies hit you, when your confidence in your own work slips, try holding on to the idea that less really can be more. Try sticking to a small range of high-quality materials and practice with them to learn how they work. Once you can use these few materials well, you *will* be able to produce every effect you want. Adopting such an approach frees you from wasting time and money chasing after every new product that comes along, and it keeps you from becoming dependent on manufacturers who are only too willing to sell you more and more stuff—much of it good for doing only one thing.

DETERMINED & NEUTRAL MATERIALS

Making any kind of art is basically the process of making a series of choices that carries out your intentions for a particular piece of work. Choosing materials and supplies is usually the first of all of these choices. Art materials can be described as falling along a continuum from neutral materials—those that don't have any meaning or much connotation of their own—to strongly determined materials—those that do carry meaning and connotations of their own.

Neutral materials include white or lightly tinted sheets of paper, standard colors of paint, blank rubber stamp-making material, ordinary black ink, colored and graphite pencils, as well as any other materials that do not assert themselves. Neutral materials will become in a sense transparent once they've been incorporated into a piece of artwork because your own expression will easily dominate them.

Strongly determined materials, at the other end of the continuum, already carry messages and connotations, and these meanings severely limit their usefulness. Consider all the nostalgic reproductions of Victorian women, children, and Renaissance angels that are sold in packages of ready-made collage materials. Originally, collage involved incorporating ephemera—the small things from everyday life that are of short-lived use or interest—into artwork. These clippings, ticket stubs, pieces of wrapping paper, and other incidental materials took on new meaning in the context of the artwork. At the same time, they brought to the work traces and hints of the original meanings and connotations that they held for the artist.

Using real ephemera from daily life can add richness to a journal. But packaged images—which might well be called pseudo-ephemera—besides not really being related to our lives have become ubiquitous, and like anything too often repeated, these images have become clichés. As such, this material weakens any artwork in which it's used unless it's radically changed or used very deliberately and for reasons that relate clearly to the concept of the piece.

WHAT TO BUY

When buying art materials, you want to know how flexible and adaptable each material will be. Are the paints of good enough quality that a few basic colors will yield good mixes? Or, must you buy the entire 30-bottle, pre-selected set because the colors are so lightly pigmented and adulterated by additives that they turn to mud when mixed? Neutral materials can be used in infinite ways and situations to do whatever needs to be done. If you decide to buy some strongly determined materials, such as pre-carved rubber stamps or stencils and printed or other decorative papers, be sure to use the meaning of the material to carry out your own intention in the artwork. Keep this material to a minimum so that it doesn't leap out— "There's that great rubber stamp of the flying fish again!"—and use it in good balance with more neutral materials.

You can, however, sometimes use determined materials ironically to great effect. For example, there's an artist's book in which the artist has used excessively cute, pre-carved rubber stamps of kittens and puppies to construct a graph of the population explosion of unwanted kittens and puppies due to failure to spay and neuter.

Following is a discussion of some basic art materials to use in your bookwork and journals. Once you understand how they work, you can decide when to buy the best and when to cut some corners. You'll also understand why materials act the way they do, so you can use them in ways that ensure they'll do what you want. As you experiment and discover new media to use in your work, always apply these tests to the materials:

- Are they of good enough quality to mix well?

- Do they result in a stable surface that won't rub off or smear?

- Will they not bleed through the particular paper you'll be using? If that's not the effect you want— don't use them.

- Are they acid free or archival?

Paper, the Substratum

Keep in mind that every material will act upon the paper to which it is applied. Therefore, before thinking about the materials you'll use on the paper, it's good to understand exactly what paper is and how it works. Knowing a few basic facts can save you a lot of time when choosing or making journals, and can help you select materials that will work well with the paper you're using.

All paper is made by first macerating, or bruising, cellulose fibers so that they will attract the water that's mixed with them to make pulp. The pulp is then formed into a sheet, and the water pressed out. Pressing causes the cellulose fibers to form hydrogen bonds with each other. The paper is then dried, and sometimes the surface is treated by pressing. Somewhere along the way, sizing is usually added, either to the pulp before the sheets are formed or to the surface of the finished sheet. Sizing is glue that stops the fibers from attracting water. The addition of sizing makes it possible to write or draw on the paper with liquid media without its bleeding through. Sometimes other chemicals are added to the paper pulp, either to improve the finish of the paper or to make it easier to form into sheets.

KIND of PAPER	SOURCE of CELLULOSE	PRODUCTION PROCESS	ADDITIVES/ SURFACE TREATMENT
inexpensive machine-made, such as newsprint or construction paper	wood pulp with impurities and high acid content; paper deteriorates quickly	large paper mill used to bruise fibers, then sheet formation by large machine and machine drying	sizing, pressing, fillers
expensive machine-made, such as good offset printing papers	100% cotton or cotton rag	same as above	sizing, hot- or cold-pressing with metal plates to give smooth or very smooth finish for some papers; calcium carbonate or other chemicals added to some to improve opacity and receptivity to ink
mold-made artists' papers	the best are 100% cotton or cotton rag yielding very strong long-lasting paper	paper mill such as Hollander beater to bruise fiber, then a cylinder-mold to form sheets	sizing; maybe cold- or hot-pressing; maybe calcium carbonate to improve opacity and to give a smooth finish for some papers
handmade decorative and artists' papers	cotton, flax, abaca, jute, hemp, sisal, kenaf, esparto, mulberry, cotton, and linen rags— many sources, all cleaned of impurities so that the paper is long-lasting	hand beaten with a mallet or stick or in a machine such as a Hollander beater; some people use kitchen blenders, but these chop and shorten fibers rather than bruise them, making the resulting paper weak	sizing; maybe pressing on variously textured blankets or surfaces or with hot irons to alter surface; maybe pigments or dyes; maybe flower parts for textural interest

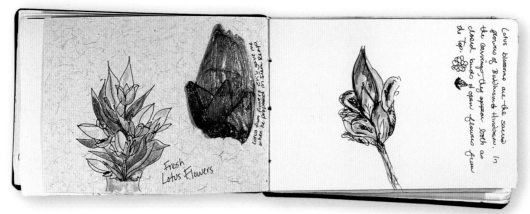

Kerstin Vogdes, *Travel Journal: Thailand and Cambodia*, 2004. 4 x 6 inches(10.2 x 15.2 cm) Hand-bound journal, PVA glue, vellum, ink, shells. Photo by Aleia Woolsey

Paper is always somewhat fragile and easily affected by what happens on its surface and even by the air around it. With this in mind, it is important to respect each sheet's limitations. Paper must be matched to the media you'll use on it. Wet media are particularly hard on paper. When you apply anything containing water to paper, you're in a sense reversing the papermaking process; the fibers of the sheet take on water to a greater or lesser degree and begin to swell, the bonds between the individual fibers weaken, and surface finishes, such as pressing, are undone to a degree.

WATERCOLOR PAPER

Whether it's mold-made, handmade, or machine-made, watercolor paper is made to withstand being wet and rewet without undue stretching and buckling. It's usually a heavier-bodied paper with sufficient sizing to control absorbency and help the matting of surface fibers stand up to scrubbing and even scratching. It comes in three main surfaces: hot-pressed, cold-pressed (also designated as "not," as in "not hot-pressed"), and rough or toothy. Hot-pressed has the smoothest, hardest surface. Cold-pressed (or not) has a slightly toothy or rough surface and is the most versatile of the three. Rough paper has a more pronounced texture. It's especially good for making bright, sparkling washes since the brush skips over some of the crevices between the bumps in the surface, leaving the white of the paper to sparkle through.

DRAWING PAPER

In addition to watercolor paper, there are a number of good-quality drawing papers sold in art supply stores made for use with pen and graphite, that also work very well with light watercolor work, such as watercolor sketching. But you must respect the limitations of this paper by not asking it to absorb as much water as watercolor paper. You can't expect a lighter paper to stand up under repeated washes, for example. But, if you just want to add light washes to pen drawings, or sketch lightly in color, drawing paper can be useful. Single-ply and double-ply bristol, a relatively inexpensive paper, is an example. Some relatively inexpensive handmade papers, such as lokta paper which originates in Nepal, are also very interesting to use for drawing as well as painting and light collage.

PAPER FOR COLLAGE

Paper that will become the base of collage needs to be heavy enough to support the weight of the elements attached to it plus the adhesive used. Lightweight paper will curl and buckle when wet adhesives are applied to it. As mentioned above, when paper is rewet, either by watercolor washes, wet adhesive, or a liquid ground, the fibers will absorb water and swell. The fibers in machine-made paper (and to some extent mold-made paper) are lined up more or less parallel to each other due to the directional movement of the papermaking machine during sheet formation. The direction of the paper fibers is referred to as the grain of the paper. (Most handmade paper does not have grain because it is shaken in all directions during sheet formation.)

When fibers in grained papers swell, they do so in a sideways direction, so that the piece of paper actually increases in size slightly in a direction perpendicular to the grain when it is wet. Then, as the paper dries and the fibers lose water to evaporation, the sheet shrinks. When paper is wet unevenly, such as when it is painted or has adhesive applied to a small part of it, it curls, buckles, and wrinkles (known as cockling) because of uneven swelling and drying. The heavier the paper and the dryer the adhesive, the flatter the paper will dry in general, unless it's stretched and dried under restraint (which is difficult to impossible to do when the paper is bound into a book). See Adhesives on page 30.

VELLUM

Translucent vellum paper is an interesting alternative to opaque sheets, but it requires some special considerations. It is made by over beating cellulose fibers to form a jelly. The pulp is then tinted, formed into sheets, and drained. The resulting paper is translucent with a smooth, low-porous surface. This paper is more reactive to moisture and temperature than conventional papers. It buckles and curls very easily when wet, so it's best to use drier adhesives on it, such as glue sticks. It can be printed on an ink-jet printer but will curl from the heat of a laser printer. You can write on it with all kinds of inks, but when you use water-based, non-permanent inks it will take a little longer to dry due to the low porosity of the paper. Watercolor, gouache, fluid acrylics, and tube acrylics will adhere to translucent paper, but they all cause some buckling and cockling. You can buy envelopes made of translucent paper, which are best glued into a journal using a glue stick.

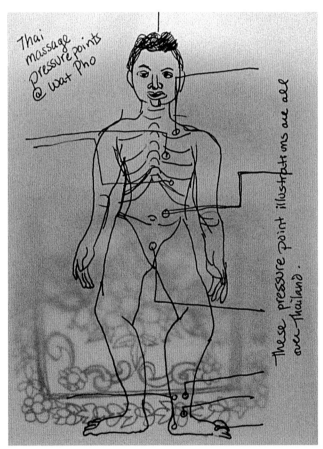

Kerstin Vogdes, *Travel Journal: Thailand and Cambodia*, 2004. 4 x 6 inches(10.2 x 15.2 cm) Hand-bound journal, PVA glue, vellum, ink, shells. Photo by Aleia Woolsey

Blank Books

Blank books, like other art materials, range from the neutral to the strongly determined. Neutral ones are generally plain and unadorned, and they pose no great challenge other than that of being blank. They can easily be made to blend with the expression of a wide variety of feelings and ideas. They can be changed, as described in the section on Customizing a Blank Book (see page 116), or they can be left as they are—whatever suits your ideas for a particular journal.

Strongly determined blank books, those made with a high level of craft, often carry much meaning of their own. They almost seem to challenge you to deface them.

Don't let them terrorize you! Always carefully consider whether a particular blank book can be made to express the feelings and ideas that you want your book to express. For example, a leather-bound book might connote traditional values of craftsmanship, elegance, and a certain formal restraint. It also offers great protection for the pages within because leather is such a strong and durable material.

14

This book might be the perfect book to turn into a travel journal, since traditional travel journals were often bound in leather. Though they were usually rather plain, travel journals were extremely durable and able to withstand being pulled in and out of a pocket or pack many times. They could also withstand the heat of the sun, desert sand, seawater, and dirt from a forest floor. And travel journals have a long tradition, making them very compatible with a traditional-looking book.

This same plain-leather book, on the other hand, could also be a great foil to a collection of riotously colored, very emotional pages that burst from within when the book is opened. The contrast between the restrained exterior and the unbridled interior can be exciting and full of meaning.

A blank book that has a cover decorated with natural materials would be an obvious good fit for a garden or wildlife journal. But its earthy-looking cover could also be an interesting juxtaposition to an interior that deals with the process of building a house, which is an example of keeping nature at bay.

An assortment of blank books

Archival Quality

There are a few other considerations to keep in mind when selecting a blank book. If you want the book to last for a long time, buy a book with acid-free or archival paper. Paper that's made from wood pulp is full of acid, and will begin to deteriorate within a few months. Look for books with labels that say they're made from 100% cotton or rag paper or acid-free paper. Some recycled paper is acid-free, but some is not, so don't assume that recycled paper is the best paper to use. Recently some manufacturers have been labeling paper "lignin free." Lignin is a natural adhesive that holds plant fibers together and gives woody plants their rigidity. Lignin is removed from fibers when fibers are cooked and cleaned prior to being beaten into pulp. But the absence of lignin doesn't itself guarantee a neutral pH. You can buy a pH-testing pen in some art supply stores. This inexpensive pen lets you make a small mark on the paper that will turn a certain color if the paper is acidic, and another color if it is neutral. This pen is a good investment because many papers are not marked as to their acidity. You can use the test pen on all kinds of papers and cardboard, including paper elements for collage.

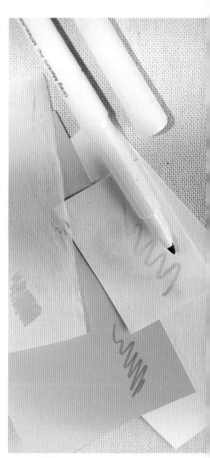

A pH pen determines that papers are acidic.

**Gwen Diehn, *Untitled Journal Page*. 6 x 9 inches (15.2 x 22.9 cm).
Pen and watercolor on handmade paper. Photo by Aleia Woolsey**

BINDING STYLES

Consider, also, the way the book is bound. Sewn bindings last a great deal longer than glued bindings. You'll be opening and closing this book often, and it needs to withstand this frequent stress on the binding.

TRADITIONAL BINDINGS

Traditional sewn bindings will stay open flat if the pages are relatively large and made of a paper that is light enough to drape. Books with closed-spine bindings afford good protection to pages as well as to other elements incorporated into the book. If you glue elements onto the pages, you can modify these books to prevent them from splaying out. (See Modifying The Book Form on pages 116 to 118.)

SPIRAL BINDINGS

Spiral or plastic comb bindings are relatively durable. They also allow the book to remain flat when open—an advantage if you work in watercolor or other wet media that must dry in an open position. The natural springiness of these bindings is also rather forgiving when you add elements to pages. When you adhere elements onto many pages, the book will still close flat instead of splaying out as it would with a tighter binding.

A stab bound journal

These bindings, however, do not afford as much protection to pages as closed-spine bindings. Because spiral bindings create a gap that separates facing pages, you may find them difficult to work with if you enjoy doing two-page spreads.

Julie Wagner, *Untitled Journal Page*, 2001. 12 x 9 x 1 inches (30.5 x 22.9 x 2.5 cm).
Spiral bound sketchbook, ink, watercolor. Photo by artist

JAPANESE STAB BINDING

Books that are sewn in the Japanese stab-binding manner (see the photo on page 16) are durable, but do not remain flat when open.

ALBUM BINDINGS

These strong bindings are related to Japanese stab bindings. They usually have some spine-thickening modifications so that they do not splay out when you glue elements to pages. They have the advantage of being able to be unbound and re-bound easily so that pages can be removed or added. These books do not generally stay flat when open.

PAPER REVISITED

The thickness and finish of the paper in a blank book should be a major concern. If you've skipped the section on paper, go back and read it now. The very thin, lightweight paper in many blank books will not accept wet media, such as acrylic or watercolor, without wrinkling and possibly tearing. Some inks and stamp pad dyes can bleed through the backs of these pages. Thin papers can also be problematic if you want to attach items to the pages. Ideally, the paper to which you glue something should be equally heavy or heavier than the elements that are attached to the page. However, in certain cases, you may prefer a thin paper. For example, you might want to emphasize the delicacy of the wildflowers you plan to draw in a nature journal. Just be aware of the limitations of thin paper, and choose the media you use with consideration of the paper's weight and delicacy.

Some blank books are made with heavy watercolor paper, and are useful if you plan to do a lot of painting in your journal. But if you want pages that drape nicely and feel soft, and you don't need all the pages to be watercolor paper, you might prefer adding some sheets of watercolor paper to a book with lighter, more graceful pages. (See Customizing a Blank Book on page 116.)

The finish of a sheet of paper refers to how smooth or rough it feels and whether or not it has had sizing added to it. Most blank books have sized paper, but if you buy one with unsized paper, you'll need to use a ballpoint, gel pen, or pencil to write in it instead of using a liquid-ink pen. In general, very smooth, hard-finished paper is not as receptive to drawing media as softer, rougher (or toothier) paper. Pigment-based stamp pad inks take a very long time to dry on hard, smooth paper, as it is not very absorbent. Experience will teach you what kinds of paper work best with the media you prefer.

Paints

All paints are made of finely ground pigments mixed in a liquid, such as water or oil, with some kind of binder added that makes the pigment adhere to a surface. Depending on the kind and quality of the paint, various other substances may be added to increase opacity or to improve the way the paint flows from a brush. In my experience, the most useful paints for bookwork are watercolor, gouache (opaque watercolors), and fluid acrylics. These are all water-based paints that dry quickly and completely, with no surface stickiness.

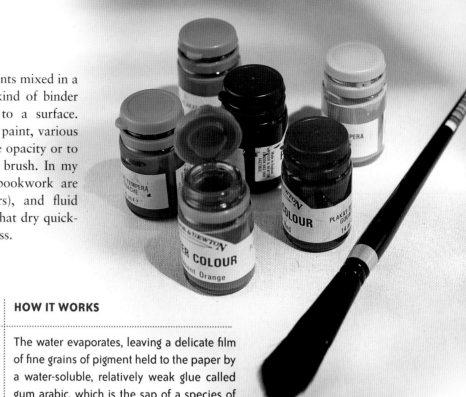

Gouache comes in both tubes and jars. These bright little jars were in a toy store and sold as poster paints, but they made fine gouache.

KIND of PAINT	BINDER	HOW IT WORKS
watercolor	gum arabic	The water evaporates, leaving a delicate film of fine grains of pigment held to the paper by a water-soluble, relatively weak glue called gum arabic, which is the sap of a species of acacia tree. Depending on the pigment, watercolors are more or less transparent. Can be rewet after drying.
gouache	gum arabic	Works exactly like watercolor. Regardless of the pigment, gouache is opaque due to the addition of China clay, talc, zinc white, or other opacifiers. Can be rewet after drying.
fluid acrylic	polymer resin	The water evaporates, leaving behind a tough film of polymer in which particles of pigment are trapped. Once dry, the polymer resin is not water soluble. Fluid acrylics are more heavily pigmented than tube acrylics. They dry completely, without the somewhat sticky surface of other acrylics, because they do not have the waxy opacifiers that are added to other acrylic paints. They are also more transparent than other acrylics, and this fact, plus their heavy pigment load, causes them to yield clean color mixes. They dilute with water and can be used to pour, drip, and stain as well as to paint.

PIGMENTS

Pigments are the coloring material in paints. They come from a variety of mineral, vegetable, and animal sources. Some are synthetic. Pigments vary in more ways than in the obvious hue or color. Some pigments, such as ultramarine, which is ground from a semi-precious stone called lapis lazuli, are rare and therefore more expensive. Others, such as yellow ochre, which comes from yellowish-brown earth or clay, are easy to find and process and are, therefore, less expensive. Some pigments are transparent and make good, clear glazes and mixes, while others are opaque and not suitable for glazing. Some are permanent and lightfast; others fade rather quickly and are referred to as fugitive.

A few bottles from among the large assortment of fluid acrylics that are available in most art supply stores

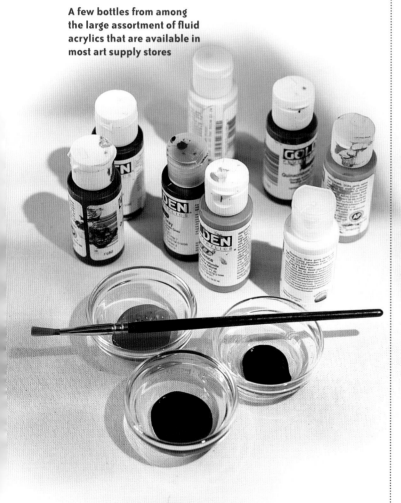

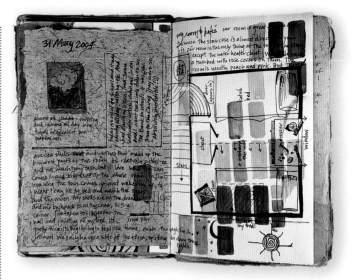

Sarah Bourne, *Ireland Journal Page*, 2004. 8^1/2 x 11 (21.6 x 27.9 cm). Hand-bound journal, handmade paper, watercolor, and ink. Photo by Aleia Woolsey

WATERCOLORS

Watercolors are manufactured in two general classes: student grade and artist's or professional grade. Artist's grade contains more pigment and fewer additives than student grade paint. The level of transparency for artist's grade is related to the transparency or opacity of the pigment, not to the addition of opacifiers or other fillers. In order to keep the price down for student grade paints, manufacturers often mix an expensive pigment, such as ultramarine, with a less expensive pigment to make a color that's similar to the pure pigment color even though it isn't an exact match. They also add opacifiers and other thickeners to student grade paint to increase the body of the paint, thereby compensating for the reduced amount of pigment.

Even if the label doesn't say artist's grade or student grade, you can tell by the price. Artist's grade paint is more expensive. It's also priced in categories determined by the cost of the pigments. Student grade paints are usually uniformly priced and contain more pigment mixes (usually labeled "hues") than pure pigment paints. Student grade paints are fine for starting out, but they don't give you the flexibility of use of artist's grade.

Watercolors come in tubes or cakes, and both are sold individually as well as in sets. If you buy tubes, you can make your own set with just the colors you want by squeezing the paint into empty pans or even into empty tin boxes such as candy tins. When you run out of a color, simply squeeze in more paint. You can mix tube paint and cake paint. If you start out with a set of cake paint and some colors run out, buy tubes of those colors and replace them as needed. Watercolors can be rewet as long as they aren't so old that the gum arabic has hardened. Even if you let watercolors dry on a palette or in their pans, they're ready to use the next time you need them by just adding water.

If you want to follow the principle of "less is more," buy only a few tubes or cakes of artist's grade watercolors. Following is a good starter list. Because artist's grade paints contain more pure pigment, these few colors will yield clear mixes and you won't have to buy lots of colors. If you buy cheap watercolors, which mix poorly, you'll need to buy many more paints in order to get a range of colors. Keep in mind that it doesn't take much paint to change a color when mixing, so mix slowly, always beginning with the lighter color and slowly adding the darker one.

WATERCOLOR STARTER PALETTE

- Cadmium yellow medium
  (an opaque, bright yellow)

- Cadmium red medium
  (an opaque, bright vermillion red)

- Permanent rose
  (a transparent, bluish-red, excellent for mixing)

- Ultramarine blue
  (a transparent, deep blue with a violet undertone)

- Cobalt blue
  (a transparent, deep blue, cooler than ultramarine)

- Raw sienna (a transparent yellowish-brown, good for glazes and mixing)

- Burnt sienna (a transparent, warm reddish-brown, good for glazing and mixing)

- Burnt umber (a warm brown, more transparent than burnt sienna, good for mixing)

Watercolors come in tubes as well as pans. The small tin shown here is an old chewing gum tin that I filled with daubs of tube watercolors to use as a small travel set. The blue-handled brushes are water brushes, an excellent tool for journal keepers on the move.

Local Pigments

A number of tailgate markets have sprung up lately in the town where I live. People seem to love eating locally for good reason—the produce is fresher, eating what's in season when it's in season gives a nice rhythm and variety to our diets, and it supports the local economy. When I travel, I especially enjoy shopping for and eating locally grown food; it's a good way to get to know a place and to feel a part of a culture, if only for a short while.

Art supplies made out of local materials can be thought of in the same way. A number of years ago I read an article about a potter who, when she traveled, always gathered a small amount of clay to make a pinch pot out of to represent the place. Journal keepers can use this idea, too. By making paints and inks out of local materials and using them in your journals, you can help represent a particular place and your experiences there.

Every place has some material that can be used to make paint, and many places have materials for making both inks and paint. Soil, especially clay-rich soil, is one almost universally available material for making paint. Take a look around; the soil in your garden may be the color of cinnamon. Across town, my friend's creek bed yields red clay, more or less the color of red bricks. There are deposits of grayish-white clay in a park near the waterfront in the village where another friend lives. In some places the local clay is so famous that it has a name. The Siena area of Italy gives its name to the colors burnt and raw sienna, while the Umbria Province of Italy gives its name to burnt and raw umber.

The word *ochre* is generally associated with a dull brownish-yellow pigment, but in fact it refers to all earth pigments. The element that all earth pigments have in common is hydrated iron oxide. It's the amount of iron oxide present that determines the color of the pigment. Ochre is, as far as we know, the most ancient pigment and the first paint. Traces of it have been found in 250,000-year-old cave paintings and in burials from thousands of years ago. Red ochres seem to have been especially prized and used for special ceremonies.

To make your own earth-pigment watercolor, begin by collecting a jar full of clay-rich soil. You can often find it near creek and riverbanks but also in road cuts as well as other places. You'll recognize clay from other soil components because its particles cling to each other, and it feels slippery and some-

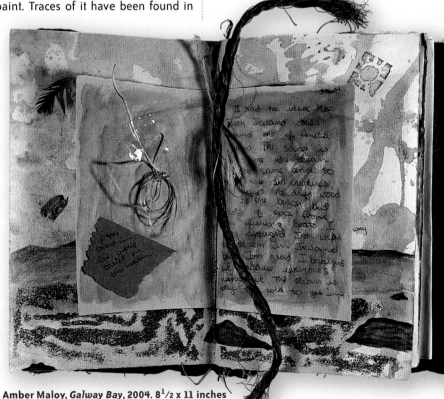

Amber Maloy, *Galway Bay*, 2004. 8¹/₂ x 11 inches (21.6 x 27.9 cm). Watercolor, watercolor pencils, pen, feather, shrimp, beach sand, rope; glued. Photo by Aleia Woolsey

what sticky when you rub it between your fingers.

Mix the clay with at least an equal amount of water. Strain the watery mix into a second container by pouring it through a layer of screen. Clean out the first container, throw away the large particles that have collected on the screen, and pour the clay-rich water (called slip) back into the first container by straining it through two layers of screen turned so that the two meshes form a finer mesh. Repeat this straining process, using finer and finer meshes. Old pantyhose are also very useful for this process.

The final straining should be done through a couple of layers of an old T-shirt. Afterward, you'll have a container of what looks like colored water. Let this stand for a few hours until you notice fine sediment settled on the bottom. Gently pour or scoop off the water, being careful to avoid stirring up the sediment. When you have poured off as much water as possible, scoop out the sediment, which is mostly pigment, onto a few layers of old newspaper. Let the remaining water evaporate. You can keep the dried lumps of pigment in a plastic bag or small bottle until you've collected enough for your project. You can store dried ochres indefinitely until you're ready to mix them with binders.

When you're ready to make paint, pour the pigment onto a smooth, hard surface (a piece of glass or marble, as well as a mortar, work very well for this process), and add enough water to make a thick paste. Grind the pigment with a blunt smooth instrument such as a pestle, the bowl of a spoon, or a dull knife until it is completely mixed with the water. Add a few drops of liquid gum arabic (available in art supply stores) as a binder to give an adhesive quality to the paint. You can store this watercolor in a regular watercolor pan. When it dries out, simply rewet it for use like any other watercolor paint.

You can also make egg tempera or casein paint out of dried pigment, depending on the binder you use. To make egg tempera, carefully separate the yolk of an egg from the white. Gently lay the intact yolk on a piece of paper towel. Lift the edges of the paper towel and carefully roll the yolk back

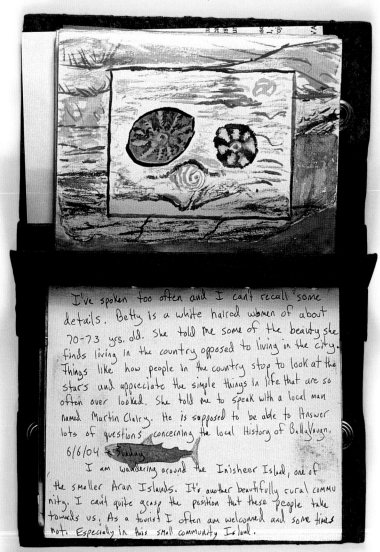

Matt Rogers, *Untitled Journal Page*, 2004. Watercolor, pen. Photo by Aleia Woolsey

and forth to remove all traces of egg white. When the yolk is clean, pinch a small bit of the yolk sack between your thumb and index finger and hold tightly while lifting the yolk. Now, feeling very Medieval, hold the yolk over a small bowl and pierce the bottom of the sack with a pin. The yolk will flow out of the sack into the bowl. To paint, dip your brush first in pigment and then in the egg yolk, being careful to avoid touching the sides of the container that has the egg yolk in it. Egg tempera has a nice, eggshell finish, giving a slightly different surface to a painting than watercolor. Be patient. You'll have to proceed slowly to build up layers of this transparent color. You can't store egg tempera, so mix just as much as you need each time you paint.

The protein in milk is called casein, and that is the part that provides the adhesive or binder in casein paint. Casein has a slight sheen, similar to egg tempera.

To make casein paint, you can mix the pigment into a little milk until the viscosity feels right for the kind of painting you want to do. Evaporated milk creates a heavy bodied paint, while skim milk will yield a more watery one.

Watercolor made from local soil pigment, and a small ink and wash painting made with this paint. The painting is of an oak gall, a source of tannin-rich pigment for making ink.

You can also make very fine ink from tannin and it ages beautifully. This local material comes from several vegetable sources, among them black walnut hulls and also the insect galls that you find on certain plants. The most tannin-rich materials are oak galls, which can be found in many locations.

Oak galls are round growths found mainly on the leaves and twigs of oak trees. They form around a growing larva after a gall wasp lays its eggs in the tissue of the plant. When the larva hatches, it drills its way out of the gall and leaves a tiny round hole, which tells you the gall is empty and the left-behind nut is rich in tannic acids. The photograph below shows a drawing of an oak gall colored with ochre. The very best galls are reputedly from shrub oaks imported from Aleppo in the Levant area of France. Perhaps you'll be going there to journal? If not, you can try galls from other oak trees to make ink. In addition to the oak galls, you'll need a half-cup or so of mild acid, such as vinegar, and a small amount of gum arabic powder or liquid.

A Medieval recipe says to crush the galls to a powder, then boil the powder in rainwater for as long as it takes to recite the *Pater Noster* three times (the whole prayer, I would assume). The vinegar is then added slowly, a few drops at a time, until the liquid turns from pale brown to black. The original recipe calls for stirring with a fig stick, but a wooden spoon or some other kind of stick works fine in my experience. The final step is to add a little gum arabic as a binder and thickener.

Another recipe for ink makes use of charcoal from your campfire or fireplace or from an oil or kerosene lantern. Collect lampblack from the glass covers of lamps (such as hurricane lanterns) or else gather a handful of charcoal. Grind the charcoal or lampblack with a mortar and pestle or with the bowl of a spoon or a spatula or table knife until it is a fine consistency. Make a solution of gum arabic and water, and grind the charcoal or lampblack into it. Dilute with more water until the ink is of the right consistency to flow from a pen. This ink darkens on the page to a beautiful bluish-black over time.

As you gain experience, you may want to add a few more colors:

- Viridian green (a cool, transparent bluish-green)

- Yellow ochre (a transparent, golden yellow)

- Payne's Gray (a cool transparent blue-gray)
  Note: Payne's gray is a hue or mix, and as such it varies from brand to brand. Experiment with different brands to find one that you like.

- Davy's Gray (a warmer opaque green-gray; also a hue or mix)

- New Gamboge Hue (a warm, bright yellow, excellent for mixing greens; another hue or mix)

- Alizarin crimson (deep bluish-red transparent, excellent for mixing but fugitive)

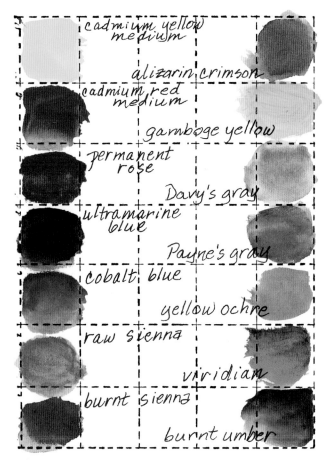

cadmium yellow medium

alizarin crimson

cadmium red medium

gamboge yellow

permanent rose

Davy's gray

ultramarine blue

Payne's gray

cobalt blue

yellow ochre

raw sienna

viridian

burnt sienna

burnt umber

A basic watercolor palette with the starter colors to the left

GOUACHE

Gouache is an opaque to semiopaque watercolor. It comes in tubes, jars, and bottles, and in a large range of colors, some of them very brilliant, but they are sometimes fugitive. For a long time, gouache was a popular medium for graphic designers who needed bright colors and a matte finish. They weren't concerned with permanence, because their work was to be photographed. Today it's relatively easy to find high-quality gouache in small sets of primary colors made for mixing—magenta (a violet-red), cyan (a greenish-blue) and yellow, as well as white and black.

Gouache varies in permanence, color, covering power, and flow from one manufacturer to another. The best quality of gouache is permanent as well as densely pigmented, which results in good covering power or opacity. The colors are pure, and good mixes are possible. It's a good idea to try out a small amount of several different brands before investing in a supply of gouache. Cheaper gouache is less heavily pigmented and relies on a white pigment, such as chalk, for its opacity and smoothness. It's difficult to get good mixes with cheap gouache, and it's often sold in sets of many colors.

Bleed-proof white is another graphic designer's paint that's sold as gouache. This very dense white paint works well as a block-out layer. It has excellent covering power, but can be rewet. If you paint on top of bleed-proof white, you'll notice some chalkiness and lightening of the color you're using as the overpaint. If you want to create a layer that won't be disturbed after it's dried, mix bleed-proof white (and any other gouache) with acrylic medium. (See Pages in Stages, page 69.)

Even if you're mainly interested in watercolors, a tube of white gouache is a good addition to your watercolor palette. White gouache mixes with watercolor to make pastels that can add nice contrast to watercolors. White gouache by itself is useful for adding highlights to watercolor sketches.

Gwen Diehn, *Untitled Journal Page*. 6 x 9 inches (15.2 x 22.9 cm).
Gouache, pen, and watercolor on handmade paper.

FLUID ACRYLICS

Acrylics come in several forms. The most popular form is in a tube and has a consistency like oil paint. You can modify it by mixing it with various acrylic mediums and gels. Over the past few years, one manufacturer of acrylics started producing a fluid form of acrylic in response to artists who wanted a pigment-saturated acrylic that could be poured, dripped, and even sprayed. The artists had been thinning traditional acrylics with water, but the resulting mix yielded weak colors. The result of the manufacturer's experiments was the finest fluid acrylics that are made today. They are so densely pigmented that they remain brilliant even when further diluted for pouring thin veils of color. Good fluid acrylics, with no added opacifiers, are the purest form of acrylic paint and are therefore excellent for mixing.

One consideration for bookwork is whether or not the surface of a dried paint is truly dry or if it's sticky. Unlike most other artwork, bookwork involves pressing paper on top of a worked surface over and over again. If a particular medium rubs off or is tacky or sticky, the artwork will eventually be harmed. Tube acrylics, depending on a

number of factors, are more or less sticky even after they're completely dry. Fluid acrylics, however, dry hard and stay that way because they contain fewer additives in the basic mix of pigment, water, and polymer resin.

All acrylics are relatively transparent, but fluid acrylics are the most transparent. You might want to buy some tube acrylics to mix with your fluid acrylics when you want more dense coverage and opacity. You can reduce the stickiness of the tube acrylics by sealing the page with a polymer varnish or by rubbing the page with a piece of waxed paper after the paint is dry.

All fluid acrylics aren't equal, and the price is largely dependent on how much actual pigment is used in the paint. There are cheap brands of fluid acrylic that are filled with additives and are made by mixing inexpensive synthetic pigments in with the more expensive pigments. In buying paint, you get what you pay for, so if you're looking for excellent color and mixing ability, buy a few bottles of the highest quality fluid acrylics and use them to mix every color you can dream of.

ACRYLIC STARTER PALETTE

- Quinacridone crimson (similar to the more fugitive alizarin crimson, a traditional violet-red mixing color; all the quinacridone colors are brilliant with vibrant undertones and excellent transparency and permanence.)

- Quinacridone gold (similar to burnt sienna yet with a golden undertone that is more brilliant than the siennas)

- Quinacridone red (a very intense mixing primary red)

- Phthalo Green/Blue Shade (transparent, deep, intense green with bluish undertones; mixed with quinacridone crimson, it yields the deepest, richest black imaginable)

- Phthalo Blue/Green Shade and Red Shade (both are transparent, vibrant blues, one cooler and the other with warm reddish undertones)

- Pyrrole Red (excellent opacity and lightfastness, similar to cadmium red, but better for mixing)

- Hansa Yellow (similar to cadmium yellow but yields clearer mixes)

- Yellow Ochre (good lightfastness; good coverage, transparent, warm brownish-yellow)

- Payne's gray (cool, bluish-gray, very dark)

To the basic palette you might enjoy adding some of the excellent metallic and iridescent fluid acrylics. The better brands of fluid acrylics include coppers, golds, and other shimmering metallics that retain their strength even when diluted with water and poured in extremely thin washes.

The acrylic starter palette

Gwen Diehn, *Untitled Journal Page*. 6 x 9 inches (15.2 x 22.9 cm). Gouache, pen, and watercolor on handmade paper. Photo by Aleia Woolsey

Brushes

A brush has a handle, bristles, and a ferrule, which is the band that holds the bristles to the handle. The bristles of the brush form a belly, which holds water, and a tip through which the water is released. A good brush has a tip that stays pointed and a well-made ferrule that prevents hairs from falling out as you work. Buying cheap brushes is a false economy. They're frustrating to work with for many reasons, but mainly because their bristles don't hold a point or even stay flat. Although good brushes can be very expensive, fortunately, as with paint, the concept of "less is more" holds true when buying them.

Two or three good brushes will serve almost any purpose for painting in a journal. You can use the same kinds of brushes for acrylics as you do for watercolor. Brushes come in rounds and flats as well as various specialty brushes such as fans, riggers, and mops. However, you don't need an array of brushes for your journal work. Just buy a #5 and a #2 round brush of good quality, such as Kolinsky sable. Over time, you can add to your collection of brushes, but you will probably find that you keep returning to your one or two old favorites.

There are three exceptions to the "good-brushes-are-expensive" rule. One of these is a recently marketed plastic-handled water brush with synthetic bristles. This very useful brush has a hollow handle for carrying water. The water is slowly released through the bristles, and, if you need a stronger flow of water, you just squeeze gently on the handle. These brushes are excellent for travel journaling because you don't need to carry extra water to use them. To clean the brush between colors, you simply wipe the bristles on a rag, paper towel, or your jeans. They come in three sizes: small, medium, and large, and also in a flat.

(right to left) Round brushes, #2 and #5, and sumi brush

You'll find a mini version (with a medium tip) for travel painting, and there's one that comes apart and can fit into a small box of watercolors. The tips are all interchangeable, so that if you want a mini with a fine tip, buy a mini and a fine and reverse the tips. The synthetic tips hold a point beautifully, and the large version of the brush is fine for laying the relatively small areas of wash that you generally do in a journal. Best of all, water brushes are reasonably priced.

Another exception is the Asian brush. Sometimes called a sumi brush, these are made with bamboo handles and are extremely inexpensive. They are wonderfully versatile, with bellies that hold a large amount of water, and tips that hold a point beautifully as long as the brush has been completely saturated prior to painting. As with any paintbrush, you must wet the entire length of the bristles when you begin to paint so that they will hold a point and not split and splay at the tip. Finally, one other inexpensive and useful brush is a 1-inch (2.5 cm) flat paintbrush that you can buy in a hardware store. It works well for laying in washes and usually costs less than a can of soda.

Water brushes

Pen and Ink

Pen and ink is a basic medium for sketchbooks and journals. The range of available pens and inks is enormous. Rather than try to describe to you what is best learned by your own experience, I will present some categories of pens and inks. Take time to find out which feel best and will make the kind of marks you want to make.

PENS

This tool is indispensable for writing, as well as for making quick sketches. Pens are capable of producing a variety of textures and tones and can be used very successfully in careful drawing. **Note:** Conventional ballpoint pens are not recommended here because they are very acidic and the ink never completely dries.

Some of the wide variety of pens and inks available

BASIC BLACK EXTRA-FINE STEEL OR PLASTIC-TIP WATERPROOF PEN

Most of these are inexpensive, last a long time, and reliably make fine, dense black lines. They produce crisp, clean lines that are useful when you want to make a precise illustration or discuss a cool, logical idea. Because the ink is waterproof, they won't bleed when you brush watercolors over them. Some brands also come in brown (sepia), blue, red, purple, and green, but usually colored inks are not waterproof.

GEL PENS

Similar to ballpoint pens, but with opaque pastel or metallic ink, these work especially well on dark papers. Most have fine tips, and many have inks that are acid-free or archival.

METALLIC PENS

All metallic pens will add a luminous quality to your pages. In the Middle Ages, silver and gold were used extensively on manuscripts to bring light into the texts they illuminated. Metallics have always carried the aura of the precious metals from which they are made. These pens come in various tip widths. The best of them—the most convincingly gold, silver, or bronze—are solvent-based and require a few minutes of shaking to mix them before use. Some will stain paper if they are incompletely mixed. Many will blot at the beginning of a line, leaving you with a glob of ink. To avoid this, keep some scratch paper at hand, and take a few strokes on it before beginning work in your journal.

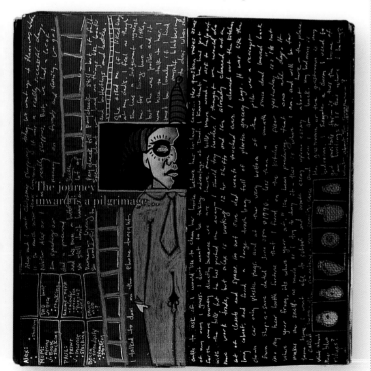

Kelcey Loomer, *Untitled Journal Page*, 2002. 12 x 11³/₄ inches (30.5 x 30 cm). Coptic bound journal, marker, silver pen, waxed linen thread, neo-pastel. Photo by Aleia Woolsey

Kelcey Loomer, *Bronze Woman*, 2004. 9¹/₄ x 6¹/₄ inches
(23.5 x 15.9 cm). Journal, acrylic paint, colored pencil, pen, email
from a friend, cut-out window; collaged. Photo by Aleia Woolsey

DIP PENS

In addition to drawing and writing with pens that have metal nibs in holders, you can use sticks, twigs, feathers, coffee stirrers, and many other objects. The marks made by this type of tool tend to be less controlled and predictable, making them more spontaneous, emotional, and lively. Experiment with Italian glass pens, thin-line crow quill pens, hand-carved bamboo reed pens. Make pens out of sticks and reeds you find at the place you're writing or drawing about. And when you discover which are best for you, keep experimenting—you'll find there's a perfect pen for every use.

INKS

There are several different kinds of ink for use with pens as well as brushes. Inks are made of ground pigments or dyes mixed in water with gum arabic added to improve flow as well as to allow the pigment to adhere to the paper after the water has evaporated. They are either waterproof or not, permanent or not.

Art supply stores sell vibrant, transparent inks in glowing colors, luminous pearlescent inks, crackling metallics, as well as jet black and smoky gray inks. Search further and you can find inks made of walnuts, wine, and oak galls. You can even make your own inks from strong coffee, teas, and beet juice. (See Local Pigments on page 21 to 22.)

WATERPROOF INKS

Waterproof inks have shellac added to them. Beware of refilling ink cartridges or fillable pens with waterproof ink because they may clog. Waterproof inks, such as India ink and some colored inks, are fine for use with dip pens, but clean the pen with water after each use. You can paint over waterproof ink with watercolor or colored ink without the waterproof-ink layer being affected.

NON-WATERPROOF INK

This ink will sink into the page more than waterproof ink and will dry to a matte finish. It's fine for line work, but you can't paint over it or it will run.

COLORED INK

Because it's made with water-soluble dyes, colored ink is not permanent or lightfast. This fugitive ink is not as problematic for bookwork as it is for work that will be exposed to light for long periods of time. However, even inside a book, colored ink will fade over time. You can dilute ink with distilled water to make washes. Inks can be mixed with each other to create new colors.

Adhesives

When you apply an adhesive to a material, the adhesive's long chain of molecules seeps into and mixes with the surface of the material, causing the adhesive to stick to the surface. When you place a second material on the material with adhesive on it, the adhesive molecules move closer together allowing the molecules of the two surfaces to attract each other and mingle, causing a strong bond between materials. While this is a very simplistic explanation of a complicated process, the important thing to realize is that using an adhesive changes the surface of the materials you're adhering. With this fact in mind, you need to approach the use of adhesives with care, since it is scarily easy to ruin a project by mishandling or choosing the wrong adhesive.

NATURAL & SYNTHETIC ADHESIVES

Natural adhesives are either plant-derived (pastes) or animal-derived (glues). Synthetic adhesives are made from polymers. Natural adhesives are made by breaking down organic substances into carbohydrates and proteins and then mixing them with water. Plant-based adhesives are more commonly used by book artists than protein- or animal-based adhesives which have largely been replaced by PVA today. Plant adhesives come in the form of pastes made from flours or starches.

Synthetic adhesives are made by manipulating single-strand molecules into multiple-strand, tacky molecules called synthetic resins. There are many kinds of synthetic resins, but the ones most useful to most book artists are polymer resins in the form of water-based polymer emulsions (PVA).

WET OR DRY?

The first thing to consider when you're choosing an adhesive is how the paper is likely to react to the water in the adhesive and whether or not you can live with the resulting changes. Since the adhesive mixes with the molecules of the paper, the paper itself becomes wet, and as it dries it cockles and buckles to a greater or lesser degree. Some papers, such as translucent papers (vellum) react strongly to water and wrinkle extensively when wet. Very thin papers tend to wrinkle and even tear in the presence of wet adhesive. Heavier papers hardly react at all. Cardboards can swell and buckle. If you've done work in water media on one side of a page, including using ink-jet ink, applying very wet adhesives to the other side of the page can cause this work to run.

As you can see on the chart on page 31, the wettest adhesives are pastes and methylcellulose, followed by PVAs (synthetic polymer-resin adhesives) and acrylic mediums (which are very similar to PVAs), followed by glue sticks (which are PVAs with much less water in them), then tape-like rolls. The driest adhesive is drymount tissue, a hot-melt adhesive tissue originally developed for use by photographers for adhering water-sensitive photographic paper to mounting boards.

Adhesives and brushes

ADHESIVE	WETNESS	GOOD FOR	DRAWBACKS
wheat or rice flour paste	very wet	relatively strong bond, non-staining, long-lasting, archival, good track record among book conservators, reversible, repositionable while wet, and it stays wet a long time, inexpensive	the gluten in wheat can attract bugs, not good for use on very thin papers and vellum, does not grab fast, very wet
wheat or rice starch paste	very wet	strong bond, non-staining, long-lasting, archival, not as attractive to insects as wheat or rice flour, smoother, reversible, repositionable while wet, slow drying	very slow drying, slightly acidic, does not grab fast, very wet
methylcellulose (made by treating wood or cotton with an alkali and then with methyl chloride)	very wet	archival, dries flexible, long shelf life in granular form, does not grow mold, non-toxic, reversible, doesn't attract pests, inexpensive, sold in granules at craft and art supply stores	weaker than flour and starch pastes, shorter track-record with conservators, very wet
PVA (comes in many forms and brands)	wet	low-odor, acid-free, non-toxic, dries flexible, strong, relatively quick bond, cleans up with water, better brands tend not to wrinkle most papers	stains leather and book cloth as well as paper, difficult to impossible to reposition or reverse, wrinkles vellum and thin papers
acrylic mediums/gels/ varnishes	wet	archival, permanent, most dry flexible, relatively strong bond, low odor, good for adhering small papers as well as top-coating and sealing items such as pressed leaves and flower parts that are adhered to pages, can be used to texture	can wrinkle thin paper and vellum, stains, can't be reversed in most cases, not good under water media, many dry tacky, use varnish only for top coating and sealing as it dries hard
glue sticks	dry	long-lasting or temporary (check the label), won't wrinkle paper, fast-drying, can adhere porous paper to non-porous surface such as mica or glass, inexpensive, doesn't attract insects, repositionable while wet	some are acidic so check labels, weak bond, some very alkaline, especially those with a strong ammonia smell
double-stick tapes	dry	some are acid-free, some are permanent, and some are repositionable (check labels); won't wrinkle paper, even vellum	very narrow band, not good for adhering large areas, expensive
drymount tissue	dry	the best are archival (these are the most expensive), non-acidic, long-lasting, can be used at home with an iron, doesn't wrinkle or cockle most papers, but the heat of the iron wrinkles vellum	can be awkward to use, requires use of a hot iron or drymount press, can't be used on heat-sensitive paper such as vellum

What is PVA?

PVA (polyvinyl acetate) is the thick white liquid adhesive that come in plastic bottles. It's marketed under a variety of names and can be school quality, craft quality, or high quality. You can tell the difference by the price. School quality PVAs are cheap. They're the kind you see sold in grocery stores in the school-supply aisle. They're low-strength and are also the most likely to wrinkle paper. They're not useful for bookwork. Craft quality PVAs are sold in craft and art supply stores and are strong, medium-quality adhesives, generally difficult to reverse, and fairly likely to wrinkle thinner papers. High-quality PVAs are usually only sold in art supply stores or outlets that specialize in bookbinders' supplies. They're usually about four times as expensive as craft-quality PVAs. They're the strongest PVAs, dry the most flexible, are the easiest to spread, and are also the least likely to wrinkle most papers. But remember that all PVAs tend to cause wrinkles when papers of unlike size, thickness, and strength are adhered to each other. All PVAs can be thinned with a little distilled water or methylcellulose to improve the way they flow from a brush, but strength is lost when these adhesives are thinned, and of course they become wetter when thinned.

PVA can also be mixed with paste. A small amount of paste increases the drying time, allowing easier repositioning.

HOW STRONG AND HOW FAST?

An important consideration when choosing an adhesive is how strong the bond needs to be. If you're just attaching a thin piece of paper to another piece of paper, you won't need a very strong bond. If you're attaching an envelope to a page, you'll need something stronger to accommodate the greater weight of the envelope as well as the stress you'll place on the adhesive bond every time you manipulate the envelope.

Related to strength is how quickly the adhesive grabs or bonds the surfaces. Some jobs, such as adhering stiff book cloth to a book cover, are much easier to do with an adhesive that grabs fast and holds tight. In other cases it's easier to use a wetter adhesive, such as paste, one that allows you to reposition several times without damaging the papers. Paste is usually used when adhering leather to boards.

OTHER CONSIDERATIONS

There are other factors to take into consideration when choosing an adhesive to use in your journal. Here are some of the most common questions to ask yourself:

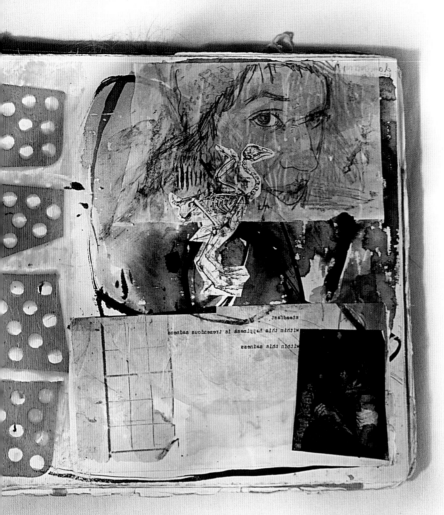

Rebecca Johnson, *Untitled Journal Page*, 2004. 11¹/₂ x 12 inches (29.2 x 30.5 cm). Handmade journal, collage with photographs, paper scraps, book pages, packaging scraps, beeswax, ink

- How quickly do I want this to dry? How tolerant of wetness are the materials to be adhered?

- Do I need a strong quick bond or will a slower one do?

- Does the adhesive attract insects, which can, of course, eventually ruin the book?

- How large are the pieces that need bonding? (PVA works best on smaller pieces)

- How convenient is the adhesive to use? If you're trying to attach things to your journal while you're flying over the ocean, a glue stick is a lot easier to use than drymount tissue (see page 34)!

- Do I need the adhesive to be forgiving of occasional clumsiness? Can it be cleaned up without staining?

- Is the adhesive reversible? Can you unattach something after the adhesive has dried?

Make Your Own Paste

Here's a good recipe for paste: Mix 1 part flour or starch with1 part water. Stir to a smooth paste. Then add 4 more parts water. Heat while stirring constantly with a wooden spoon over medium heat (a double boiler is usually suggested, but not necessary if you keep the heat low enough and stir constantly). When the paste first comes to a boil, count to 30 and then remove it from the heat. Option: Add a few drops of essential oil such as lavender or rosemary to make it a little less attractive to molds and insects and to give it a good smell as well as the vibrations of the plants from which the oil was made. Store the paste in a covered jar, labeled with the date, in a refrigerator. Keeps for about a week. Best used when fresh and still warm.

It can be rewarmed by sitting it in the sun or near a heater.

Drymount Tissue

Drymount tissue can be found at photographic supply stores. It comes in several grades, with the most expensive being the thinnest with the best archival qualities. When you use it to laminate two sheets of paper together, the resulting laminate will be stiffer and more like card stock than the individual pieces. This can be an advantage or a disadvantage, depending on the project. Originally designed to be used in a drymount press, it works fine if you place it between the two sheets to be adhered and iron the papers for a few seconds to a minute with a warm (not hot) iron with no steam. It's a good idea to cover the top sheet with scrap paper. The piece of drymount tissue should be cut to fit ⅛ inch (3 mm) inside the perimeter of the papers being laminated. (See Laminating Pages on page 117.)

APPLICATION OF ADHESIVES

Liquid PVAs and pastes are applied with brushes, and you'll want to keep one brush for PVAs and a different one for pastes—PVAs are harder on brushes and will stiffen them over time. Ideally, paste brushes should be softer, more tapered, and more flexible than PVA brushes. To apply paste, stroke the paste onto the paper to be adhered for several minutes to allow the paste to penetrate and soak the paper. At first the paper will curl. Continue brushing until it lies flat again. Then apply the item to the dry page. To apply PVA, use a stiff, blunt brush to push the PVA into the paper. You don't need a lot of force, but will need more of a pounding motion than the stroking motion you use for paste. Work as quickly as possible, as the PVA dries much faster than paste.

BASIC ADHESIVE SELECTION

Depending on the kind of paper you generally use, a basic adhesive kit would include a bag of wheat or rice flour (ground very fine) or starch for making paste (which you can use as both adhesive and sizing), a pH-neutral glue stick, and a bottle of the best PVA you can afford. To that add one paste brush and one PVA brush and an old telephone directory to use as scrap paper when you use your adhesives. From time to time you may want or need one of the other adhesives, but you can go for a long time with the basics.

RUBBER CEMENT AND TAPES

You'll notice that rubber cement and tapes of all kinds were not included in this discussion. Rubber cement is a solvent-based wet adhesive. It forms a strong, flexible bond and doesn't wrinkle papers. But it was not designed to be permanent, and the bond weakens with age (and not very much age at that). Its solvent base is toxic and damages paper over time—the solvent base can harm some papers and photographs immediately. It's not recommended for permanent work.

Tapes are a form of pressure-sensitive adhesive. These are generally not very strong, and they lose their adhesive qualities as they dry out over time. Even if they are sold as "acid free," they eventually discolor and deteriorate paper. There are a few tapes, such as linen tape, that are archival and approved by some conservators, and if you feel that you must use tape, look for these in bookbinding- and matting and framing supply catalogues.

Does this mean you should never indulge in the fun of using masking tape or Band-Aids or duct tape in your journal? Of course not!

Pencils and Crayons

What could be easier to buy and use? While you might be thinking of more sophisticated art supplies, don't overlook these versatile and simple tools that can create many wonderful effects on their own.

GRAPHITE PENCILS

These are excellent for rendering subtle differences of dark or light as well as a variety of textures. They can make very gentle, graceful marks or crisp, precise ones depending on the technique used.

Graphite pencils are graded and sold according to the ratio of graphite to binder that determines their range of hardness. Softer pencils that have a less waxy binder make darker marks and smear easily. The softer pencils are the "B" pencils, and the higher the number before the B, the softer the pencil. Harder pencils are called "H" pencils, and the higher the number the harder the pencil. Since you want to avoid using materials that will smear for journal work, stay away from extremely soft pencils. A good range is between 3B and 2H. Keep a pencil sharpener and sandpaper block handy to sharpen your pencils.

Some graphite pencils are made with a water-soluble binder. These will make a wash when you brush the pencil lines with water. Even regular graphite pencil lines can be turned into washes by using mineral spirits and a brush.

Watercolor pencils

WATER-SOLUBLE COLORED PENCILS

Although water-soluble colored pencils tend to be slightly lower in intensity and brightness than waxy colored pencils, they dry hard and won't smear or rub off onto facing pages like the waxy ones do. You can use them for writing and drawing, or you can apply them on a page using broad strokes to create layers of color. These layers can then be turned into washes by brushing them with a wet brush. You can then apply more color if you wish or create textures on top of the washes. If you must use waxy colored pencils, place tracing paper or vellum between the pages to interleaf them to prevent the colors from smearing or rubbing off on the facing page. You can also try waxing the page with balled-up waxed paper.

Wendy Hale Davis, Sabado/Leap, 2004.
(8 x 17 1/2 inches 20.3 x 44.5 cm). Ink, watercolor, crayons, acrylic
paint. Photo by Anne Butler

CRAYONS

Because crayons aren't good for rendering small detail,
they're always a somewhat abstract medium. For the best
effect, use them to communicate generalized information
with bold strokes or to create fields of color.

In addition to your basic wax crayons, art supply
stores also sell water-soluble crayons. Both kinds are useful to the journaler. You can use regular wax crayons for
the process of wax resist. To do this, first use a light colored crayon to draw a shape or shapes. Then brush
watercolor washes over the shape and its background.
The watercolor will adhere only to the non-waxy areas of
the paper, yielding an interesting surface that can look
something like batik.

Water-soluble crayons work just like water-soluble colored pencils but they have thicker points. They also
deposit a heavier layer of pigment onto the paper, and
when you brush over them with water, the resulting surface is somewhat grainy, which adds an interesting texture. Oil pastels are also fun. Their soft creamy texture
allows you to use your fingers for mixing right on
the page.

Water-soluble crayons

Other Useful Tools

STENCILS

Because text is an important design and communicative element, you can broaden the range of lettering on your pages by using various guides or stencils. You can find these at craft, drafting, or office supply stores. Choose different fonts or letter styles so that you'll have ones that suit a variety of moods or purposes. You can also use the stencil for the basic letter shape, and then tailor the letters to the project at hand.

MATT KNIVES

These are useful for removing pages, shaping pages and corners, and trimming ephemera for use in collage. The heavy-duty kind with break-off blades is the most flexible and therefore useful. Invest in one of these rather than buying the smaller, flimsier ones sold in most craft stores.

You may have to go to a hardware store for it. Get a few extra packs of blades while you're at it.

STRAIGHTEDGES

If you plan to make your own journals, a good steel straightedge is a worthwhile investment. Steel is harder than aluminum and will resist cuts that result from slips of the blade. Although these straightedges are expensive, they last forever and are useful for tearing as well as cutting paper and board. If you can get a 36-inch-long (1 m) steel one with one beveled edge and one straight edge, you'll be in business. If you want a good, general-use straightedge first for drawing lines, get a 12-inch (30.5 cm) aluminum one. This is an inexpensive item, but also one that will last forever.

Andrea A. Peterson, *Ox Bow*, 2003. 12 x 18 inches (30.5 x 45.7 cm). Coptic hand-bound journal, cotton rag handmade paper, pastel chalk, toothpicks, colored pencil, handmade paper; glue. Photo by artist

Grounds

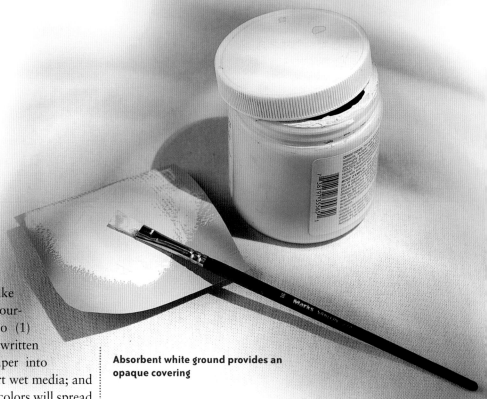

Absorbent white ground provides an opaque covering

Book artists, especially people who make altered books or who use old books as journals, are always looking for ways to (1) opaque out material already printed or written on the page; (2) transform flimsy paper into something substantial enough to support wet media; and (3) improve the paper's surface so watercolors will spread better and look brighter, and pen and strange experimental media (such as shellac) won't bleed through and stain the other side.

I would love to be able to write that you can easily turn flimsy or aged paper into strong, useful paper by applying one of the many grounds available to artists. But acrylic gesso, absorbent ground, wheat paste, gelatin, even traditional animal-glue gesso, as well as acrylic mediums and gels all have limited use in transforming paper. I have spent a lot of time trying out all of these substances on a variety of papers, both single sheets and in journals and old books. So far what I've learned is that all of these substances are wet, and they all make the papers curl and crinkle to some degree. Some papers dry flatter than others (but these are always the heavier papers that don't need transforming in the first place). In no case have I been able to turn a flimsy piece of paper into a good page for water media.

However, in trying to find solutions to this problem, I've come up with a few things that do work. Wheat paste and gelatin sizing, especially when applied to heavyweight paper, can reduce the absorbency of the paper to a degree and thereby make watercolors and inks look a little brighter. This is because the pigments are not sinking into the paper as much, but are sitting more on the surface and therefore are showing up more.

Absorbent ground is an acrylic product that I've found is the best for blocking out. It dries to a porous, paperlike surface and even turns glossy surfaces into surfaces that can receive any media that paper can hold. You can use acrylic absorbent ground to block out the print in a book you're altering, but sadly the resulting surface is not as good for watercolor or pen as plain paper. The absorbent ground can be an interesting surface, by appying it thickly and then engraving it after it's almost dry. Water-based media adhere to it better than they do to acrylic gesso, but don't expect to be able to create a true paper-like surface for delicate work.

Tara Chickey, *Untitled Journal Page*, 2003.
10 x 20 inches (25.4 x 50.8 cm). Spiral-bound journal, handmade silk paper, watercolor paper, gesso, acrylic paint, 24-gauge copper wire, pen, alphabet rubber stamps, alphabet stickers.
Photo by artist

Acrylic gesso is also an acrylic-based product, but it produces a slightly glossy surface that is not as good for wet media as absorbent ground. Acrylic gesso is of limited use in blocking out underlying text because it's relatively transparent. It also produces a non-porous surface that's not a suitable ground for watercolors or pen and inks. However, it can be used under fluid acrylics provided the paper is heavy enough to support the heavy surface that will result from the layers of denser medium. Another material that blocks out an underlayer is gouache (see page 24). But because it's water soluble, the resulting surface is subject to being rewet and anything you paint over it will mix with the gouache.

If the old page is very thin and subject to wrinkling with wet adhesive, you can laminate other paper (see page 117) over the print in an old book using glue stick; if the page is heavier, try laminating and collaging with PVA.

How Does Your Journal See the World?

Art always tells us something about how its maker understands the world. For example, artists who lived in 16th-century Europe, at the time of the Renaissance, represented the world by carefully rendering its material details from a fixed perspective, a single vantage point. Paintings were like windows onto scenes of exquisite naturalism. Painters were reflecting a worldview in which people saw the material world as fixed and certain, and they believed their truths to be absolute. They enjoyed new-found control over the world, thanks to new discoveries by explorers and scientists, and they felt confidently placed at the center of the universe.

A few centuries earlier, during the Middle Ages, people did not consider the material world to be so important. Instead, the earthly world was seen as merely a prelude to the afterlife of the spirit. Accordingly, the figures in Byzantine church mosaics seem to float in an unearthly space of color and light, surrounded by golden halos or auras. All of the figures look like members of a large extended family who shared genes for almond-shaped eyes, elongated bodies, dark curling hair, and tiny, insubstantial feet that seem incapable of bearing the weight of the bodies, much less moving them around. They live in an indeterminate space, and their eyes are fixed on the world beyond the senses.

It's interesting to tease apart the different strands that make up our current expression. In our artwork today, we borrow from many different traditions because we have access to so much of the past as well as the work of other cultures. When we allow ourselves to try on different ways of seeing as we work in our journals, we can enrich our practices as well as increase our appreciation of the variety that surrounds us.

Journals, those strange amalgams of image and text, utilitarian purpose and art, also reflect the interests and values—the worldview—of the people who produce them. Considering different ways of making sense of the world can help you enlarge your journal practice. In this section we'll look at seven different ways of seeing the world and reflecting those visions in a journal.

Sarah A. Bourne, *Ireland Journal Page*, 2004. 8¹/₂ x 11 inches (21.6 x 27.9 cm). Hand-bound journal, handmade paper, watercolor, ink. Photo by Aleia Woolsey

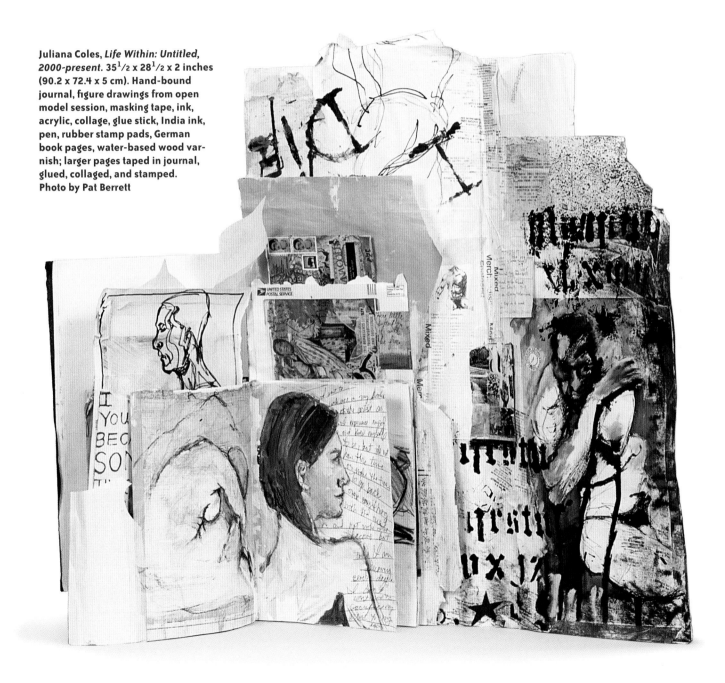

Juliana Coles, *Life Within: Untitled,
2000-present.* 35^1/$_2$ x 28^1/$_2$ x 2 inches
(90.2 x 72.4 x 5 cm). Hand-bound
journal, figure drawings from open
model session, masking tape, ink,
acrylic, collage, glue stick, India ink,
pen, rubber stamp pads, German
book pages, water-based wood varnish; larger pages taped in journal,
glued, collaged, and stamped.
Photo by Pat Berrett

The Layered World

The Layered World

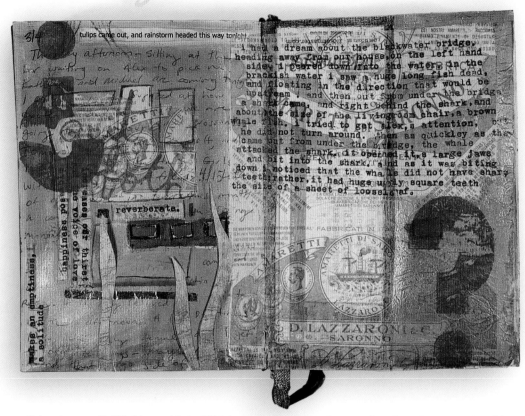

Kelcey Loomer, *Untitled Journal Page*, 2004. Journal, typewritten dream and quote on transparent cookie wrappers from Italy, pastels, ink, PVA glue, gold acrylic paint; collaged. Photo by Aleia Woolsey

Why are so many of us crazy about layers these days? Is it simply because it's easy to work in layers on a computer, making the layered look fashionable in graphic design? Clearly there's more to it than layers simply looking good to many people. Maybe it's because layers are a kind of visual equivalent of talking on a cell phone, while driving in traffic, while listening to the radio and answering kids' questions, while trying to keep from spilling a cup of hot tea. It's the quintessential post-post-modern lifestyle—lots of things going on at the same time.

Artists working in layers today represent a world that they see as existing on many different levels: one that is constructed differently by individuals and diverse groups of people all at the same time. Layers can represent different levels of meaning in the world as well as in the piece of artwork. They show how one event can color the others around it, how one meaning changes as it intersects with others, how nothing is simple and nothing stays the same. They show the randomness that causes interesting things to happen when two layers generate a third set of images that no one could have predicted.

Creating the Illusion of Layers

To produce the illusion of layers in a journal you need transparency and translucency so that it's possible to see more than one layer at a time. You also need bottom layers that stay put once they're on the paper. The main characteristics of a transparent medium are the absence of fillers and opacifiers, and the presence of transparent pigments. The main characteristic of a permanent medium is that when its water evaporates, its binder is no longer water soluble. Therefore, it glues the pigment to the paper permanently and won't let it move around when another water medium is placed on top of it.

You can begin working in layers by writing, drawing, painting, printing, or pouring the bottom layer with a waterproof medium. Some waterproof mediums are graphite and wax-based colored pencils, acrylics, waterproof pens—colored gel pens as well as black ones—wax crayons, and varnish-based or other waterproof inks, copier transfers, and some stamp-pad inks. Collage items are often waterproof, especially color copies and scraps of commercially printed images and text. It's important to let the bottom layer dry thoroughly before working over it if you want to create the effect of transparency when you add the top layer.

Some transparent materials that are suitable for use in books are fluid acrylics, acrylic mediums, watercolors, water-soluble crayons and pastels, inks, and translucent or transparent papers such as vellum, some oriental papers,

Figure 1

acrylic over copier transfer

watercolor over wax crayon and graphite

inks over graphite

acrylic over acrylic

watercolor over poured acrylic

ink over poured acrylic

tissue over acrylic, ink over acrylic

tissue over acrylic, ink over black pen

watercolor crayon over wax crayon

acrylic over waxy colored pencil

watercolor over permanent ink

ink over stamp pad

Figure 2

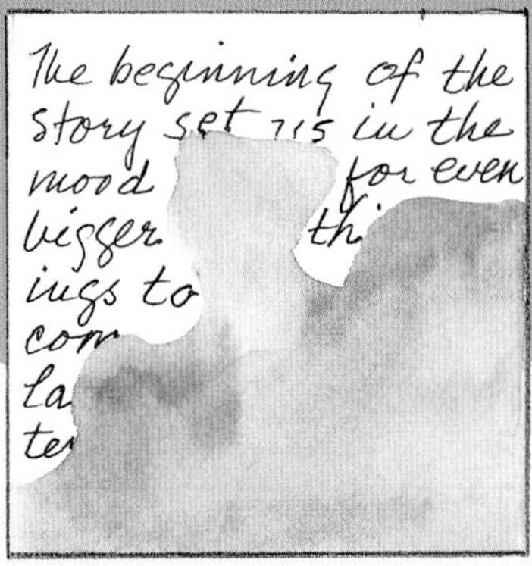

Figure 3

and thin tissues. Figure 1 on page 43 shows a variety of waterproof bases with different transparent top layers applied. Experiment and you'll discover which combinations you like best. By remembering the principles outlined above, you'll also figure out other materials to use and other ways to generate the effect of layers.

In addition to actually layering art mediums, you can get the effect of layers by placing materials on a page in such as way that they appear to be in layers. One way to do this is to write or draw right up to the edge of another element on the page so that the writing or drawing appears to pass under the second element, as shown in figure 2. Another way to create the appearance of layers is to use small amounts of an opaque medium, such as gouache, to make areas seem to come forward from the bottom layer. This works especially well if you then add transparent shadows to the opaque elements, as shown in figure 3.

The Creative World

"Creative" is one of those overused words that pops up in the most banal of settings: "Be creative! Flambé those bananas!" And, "Now you too can create the environment you want using our new Kreatif Kolors to sponge paint your walls. Follow these easy directions..." The *Oxford English Dictionary* defines creation as "The action of making, forming, producing, or constituting for the first time or afresh; invention; causation; production," and it is in this sense that I use the word here.

Leonardo Da Vinci's notebooks or journals are often cited when the word creative comes up. They're well known for many reasons. For starters, we all know that he wrote in mirror writing. We also know that he described and even invented many things centuries before the rest of the world got around to thinking about them—flying machines, submarines, farm machinery, and even instruments for various surgical procedures. His journals have been appreciated as much for the beauty of his drawings, with their lovely inscrutable filigree of text, as for the ideas expressed. These are creative journals in the original sense of the term.

Because Leonardo reflected the worldview of the Italian Renaissance—a world possessing order, one capable of being perfectible—you won't find him whining about his relationships in the pages of his journals. No ecstatic travelogues either. When he does describe a natural phenomenon (e.g., a baby in utero or a river system), it's with the intention of discovery and disclosure.

Many artists and inventors use their journals in this way. Stage and costume designers, poets and writers, painters, choreographers, and musicians often keep notebooks close at hand for a daily updating of their ideas. Teachers have their plan books; inventors have their notebooks; and I once saw a carpenter's lovely hand-

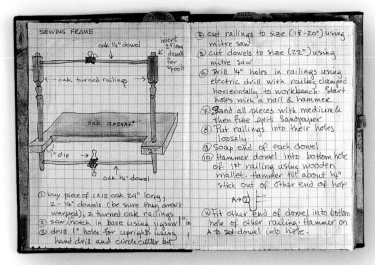

Gwen Diehn, *Untitled Journal Page*. 5 x 6¹/₂ inches (12.7 x 16.5 cm). Coptic journal, handbound by Sandy Webster, watercolor and pen. Photo by Aleia Woolsey

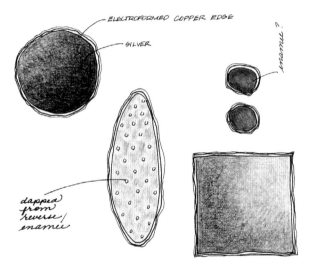

Billy Jean Theide, *Edges*, 2004. 8¹/₂ x 11 (21.6 x 27.9 cm). Hand-bound journal, sketch paper, ink, colored pencils. Photo by the artist

made, leather-wrapped, grid-paper notebook. In it, he kept detailed sketches of all his projects along with notes about materials, costs, construction problems, and solutions. He used a flat, wooden carpenter's pencil for his drawings and notes, and he rolled pencil and sewn-together text pages in a wrap-around cover, a well-used rectangle of leather, which he stuck in his back pocket.

A creative journal focuses on the future and how to get there. It's a tool of the imagination, but it's also a means for realizing dreams and plans. This is a journal that goes along to the hardware store, or the garden center, or the junkyard. If you work near water, it may get wet. If you work in a garage or workshop, it may get greasy.

This journal needs to be weatherproof and sturdy! Leather or heavy canvas are ideal cover materials. A waterproof pen or a graphite pencil makes sense as a medium for working in it. Quadrille or grid paper as well as a supply of tracing vellum tucked into the back pages may be handy. Colored inks can be useful in making diagrams, maps, and drawings, but these should be varnish- or acrylic-based in order to withstand hard use and occasional overnights outside on a damp work site. I've seen waterproof quadrille paper designed for surveyors who must often work in the

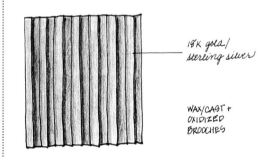

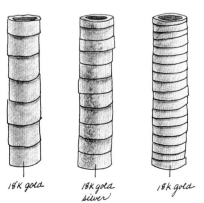

Billie Jean Theide, *Stripes*, 2004. 11 x 8¹/₂ inches (27.9 x 21.6 cm) Hand-bound journal sketch, paper, ink, colored pencils. Photo by artist

45

rain. But the water-repellent surface also repels liquid ink and water media. It's okay for graphite, but that's about it. If you know you're going to be working in your journal while standing in a drizzle, and you're content to limit yourself to graphite, you might look for this paper to use in making your journal. I found it in a bookstore, but I imagine drafting supply stores would be a more likely source.

Whatever the materials, the contents of this journal will always be enormously useful. While the practical information in the journal will help you work out the details of current projects, the journal can also become a repository for ideas for future projects. You might keep a section in the back just for jotting notes and making sketches of glimmerings of ideas, thoughts that you don't want to lose but that you haven't yet figured out what to do with. Someday, when you refer back to the journal, one of those sketches may well become the seed of your next project.

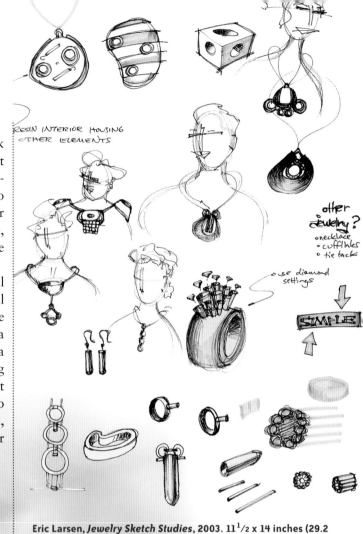

Eric Larsen, *Jewelry Sketch Studies*, 2003. 11¹/₂ x 14 inches (29.2 x 35.6 cm). Hand-bound journal, marker, ink.
Photo by the artist

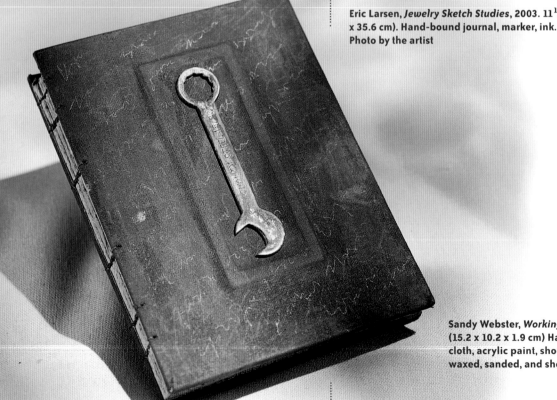

Sandy Webster, *Working Journal Series*, 2000. 6 x 4 x ³/₄ in. (15.2 x 10.2 x 1.9 cm) Hand-bound journal, papers, book cloth, acrylic paint, shoe polish, wrench; glued, painted, waxed, sanded, and shellacked.

Brains on Paper

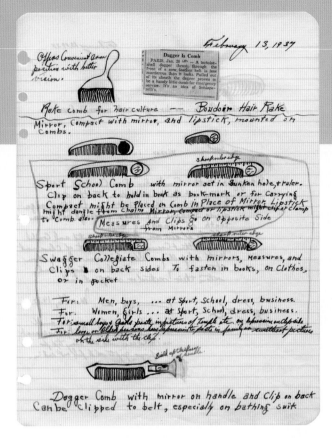

February 13, 1937

Offers Convenient arm position with better Incision.

Dagger Is Comb
PARIS, Jan. 20 (P) — A tortoise-shell dagger thrust through the front of a new feather belt is less murderous than it looks. Pulled out of its sheath the dagger proves to be a handy little comb for emergency service. It's an idea of Schiaparelli's.

Rake comb for hair culture — Boudoir Hair Rake

Mirror, Compact with mirror, and lipstick, mounted on Combs.

Sport School Comb with mirror set in Sunken hole, + ruler. Clip on back to hold in book as book-mark or for Carrying Compact might be Placed on Comb in Place of Mirror, Lipstick might dangle from Chain Mirror, compact or lipstick might clip at clamp to Comb also.

Measures And Clips go on Opposite Side from Mirrors

Swagger Collegiate Combs with mirrors, measures, and Clips on back sides To fasten in books, on Clothes, or in pocket

For: Men, boys, ... at Sport, School, dress, business.
For: Women, Girls, ... at Sport, School, dress, business.
For: small boys ...
For: ...

Dagger Comb with mirror on handle and Clip on back Can be Clipped to belt, especially on bathing suit

Journals have always played a big part in inventors' lives. They're the nets that catch new ideas and hold them gently while the inventor fine-tunes, modifies, erases, adds on, and sometimes even admits to being unsure, puzzled, or at a dead end. One of Charles Darwin's notebook pages contains a tree diagram with text in which he speculates on the theory of evolution. At the top of the page Darwin has written two words: "I think."

Earl Tupper was a journal keeper who was an unlikely candidate to make a million before he was 30. Poor and uneducated beyond high school, he had grown up on a small family farm in New England. His father tinkered about to invent laborsaving devices for the farm and greenhouse, such as a frame to help in the cleaning of chicken houses. It was from watching his father design these items that Earl began to see the path that would lead him to his fortune.

When Earl graduated from high school in 1925, he worked on the farm for a couple of years, then took on a number of different jobs, including work as a mail clerk and a job on a railroad labor crew. In 1928 he studied tree surgery and set up his own business, which he and his wife ran throughout the early 1930s. The income from this business enabled Tupper to continue to play around with ideas for inventions that he had pursued from boyhood. Even after Tupper Tree Doctors failed in 1936, Tupper remained confident that he could make a living from some of his inventions.

While inventing was the thread that ran through Tupper's life, the repositories of his ideas were his invention notebooks or journals. These are wonderful examples of a brain on paper, and they span much of his lifetime. They give us a glimpse into the thought processes of the inventor, recording not only the spectacular successes—such as his work with plastics that led to the invention of the Wonderbowl with the Tupper seal and to the refinement of plastic that became Tupperware—but also all the near-misses and spectacular failures that were part of the risk-taking an inventor goes through on the road to success.

Tupper never stopped inventing. He carried little pads of paper in his shirt pocket for getting his ideas down when they came to him. These he copied into his invention notebooks, a set of looseleaf binders filled with his drawings, explanations, and revisions. His ideas included a fish-powered boat, a no-drip cone for ice cream, a fishing pole with built-in scale for weighing the catch, a belt buckle into which a photograph could be pasted, a folding comb that he called a dagger comb (shown above), and a waterproof watch, which he called a water bracelet. Long after selling the Tupperware Company for $16,000,000 in 1968, Tupper was still hard at work, coming up with inventions and ideas for products.

One of Tupper's later notebook pages contains a design for a device (made out of two modified Tupperware rolling pins) that was to be used for washing clothes in a motel. The traveler would not only be able to wash small items of clothing, but would also get his exercise by performing a series of maneuvers for which Tupper would provide a description to accompany the product. At the end of the process, the traveler not only had clean underwear, but he had also had a good workout and would sleep soundly while his clothes dried over the back of the motel's desk chair.

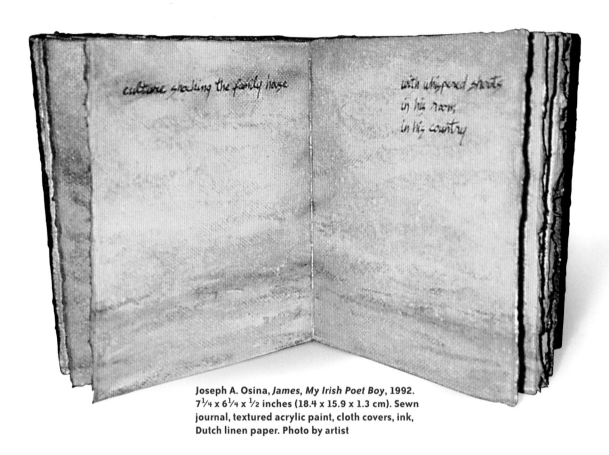

Joseph A. Osina, *James, My Irish Poet Boy*, 1992.
7¼ x 6¼ x ½ inches (18.4 x 15.9 x 1.3 cm). Sewn
journal, textured acrylic paint, cloth covers, ink,
Dutch linen paper. Photo by artist

The Japanese aesthetic of wabi-sabi is a nature-based idea that is very much the opposite of the materialistic aesthetic of our digitized world. It's also very different from the rich complications of the layered world. While it's difficult to define wabi-sabi, Leonard Koren comes close in his book *Wabi-Sabi for Artists, Designers, Poets, and Philosophers* (1994, Stone Bridge Press, Berkeley, CA). when he says, "Wabi-sabi is a beauty of things imperfect, impermanent, and incomplete. It is a beauty of things modest and humble. It is a beauty of things unconventional."

Wabi-sabi is closely aligned with the qualities of simplicity, the transience of life, and a lack of perfection. Wabi-sabi materials are natural and often corroded in such a way as to be richer and more poignant because of their degradation. In the wabi-sabi worldview one arrives at truth by observing nature, especially its inconspicuous and often overlooked details. Wabi-sabi teaches that beauty can come from ugliness and from acceptance that life is fleeting and always changing.

A wabi-sabi journal might be the focal point of a practice in which you seek to simplify your life, where you begin to find meaning and beauty in unadorned events and objects. It can be a tool that helps you come to terms with the fleeting quality of life while relaxing into an enjoyment of the passing parade. Accordingly, wabi-sabi materials are those that suggest erosion and other natural processes—the irregular, the earthy and unpretentious, the intimate.

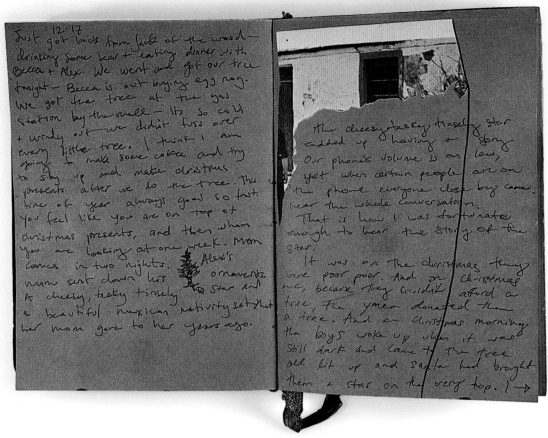

Kelcey Loomer, *Untitled Journal Page*, 2002. 12 x 11³/₄ inches (30.5 x 30 cm).
Pen, collage. Photo by Aleia Woolsey

Wabi-sabi colors are generally warm, dark, and low in intensity. (Think of a soft, faded, apricot-colored brick wall with a few fragments of paper and a rusty staple left behind from a long-gone poster.) A slightly crooked clay pot on a rough, wooden bench is infinitely more wabi-sabi than a Ming Dynasty Chinese bowl on a gleaming mahogany end table.

The wabi-sabi journal, then, is one that's simple rather than elaborate, rough rather than smooth—and certainly never slick. It will be made of natural materials to remind us of the change that's constant in nature despite our efforts to hold onto things and to preserve the present for the future. Flour paste, handmade papers, cloth, and leather come to mind, as well as humble natural elements such as leaves or a feather. The mediums used will be minimal: a pen with black ink, a soft graphite pencil, some warm washes of grays and tans, perhaps made from local clay pigments. Some pages might be prepared by pouring strong tea or coffee on them. Collage elements will not only be simple, but will be beautifully and thoughtfully arranged. A single small spot of color might accentuate an otherwise empty page.

Opacity is a useful quality in a wabi-sabi journal. A wash of white gouache can soften elements on a page like a fine layer of clouds can soften the landscape seen from a mountaintop. A thick layer of acrylic absorbent ground can furnish a base that can be loosely engraved with words or images that need no added color. Multiple layers of absorbent ground and thin paper can create a peeling or decaying look.

Coloring the Wabi-Sabi World

Since wabi-sabi colors tend to be low in intensity, a little knowledge of color theory can be useful when you need to dull an overly bright green or take away the bite from a particularly acid yellow. A color wheel is an easily constructed tool that you can use as a reference whenever you want to mix colors. By making your own color wheel from the paints you'll actually use, you can get an accurate picture of your available palette.

Using the most transparent watercolors or fluid acrylics that you have, begin by painting three spots of color arranged in a triangle. Put a spot of blue (ultramarine works well, or pthalo blue) at the top, then a spot of clear, lemony yellow to the right and below the blue, then a spot of magenta, or dark pinkish-purple red to the left and below the blue (see figure 1).

Next, mix a very little bit of the blue with a brush load of the yellow in order to get a clear green. Paint that between the blue and yellow spots. Mix a small bit of magenta into a brush full of yellow to get a bright orange. Paint the orange between the magenta and the yellow. Finally, mix equal amounts of magenta and blue to get a violet or purple. Paint that between the magenta and the blue (see figure 2). This is your basic color wheel showing primary and secondary colors. Now the fun begins.

Jeanne G. Germani, *Untitled Journal Page*, 2003. 9 x 8¹/₄ x ¹/₂ inches (22.9 x 21 x 1.3 cm). Altered book, acrylic paint, PVA, vintage decorative piece; painted, glued. Photo by artist

There are two basic principles of color theory that will serve you very well:

• Complementary colors are the colors opposite each other on the color wheel: red (or magenta) and green, blue and orange, purple and yellow. When these are mixed together, they lower each other's intensity. For example, if you want to dull that grass-green, add a small amount of red (magenta) to it and watch the intensity drop. If you want to make your red a little less cherry-like, add a small bit of green, and so on.

• However, complementary colors intensify each other when they are placed side by side. If you want a blue to really stand out or "pop" for example, put a spot of orange next to it or in the middle of it and watch the intensity of both colors rise.

Another skill that color theory helps you with is the mixing of subtle grays, which is very important for working in a wabi-sabi manner. Taking the principle that complementary colors mixed together lower each other's intensity to its extreme, complementary colors can be mixed and balanced carefully so that the mix yields a very

Figure 1 *Figure 2* *Figure 3*

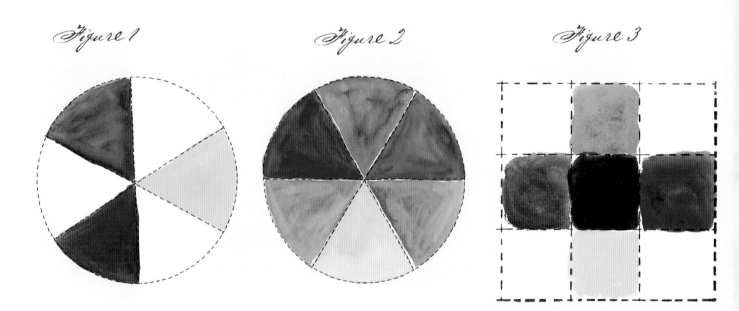

Figure 4

beautiful neutral gray. You can mix far more nuanced grays using complementary colors than you can by mixing black and white. If you want a warm gray, try mixing red and green. If you want a cooler gray, try blue and orange or purple and yellow (see figure 4).

You can use the same principle to mix the richest blacks imaginable (see figure 3). To mix black, start with ultramarine or pthalo blue and add magenta to it until you have a very dark violet. Then add a very small bit of yellow to warm up and neutralize the violet. You can cool down the black by adding more blue, or warm it up by adding more red (magenta).

A muted wabi-sabi range of colors is shown in contrast between more intense counterparts.

The Naturalist's World

The Naturalist's World

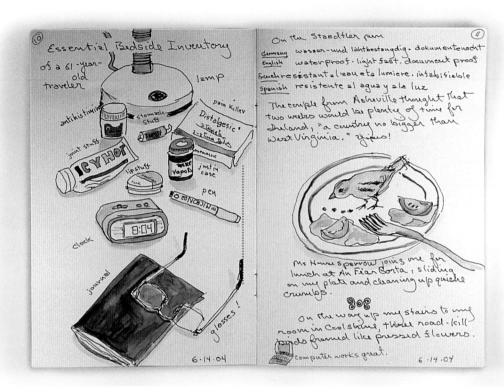

Ann Turkle, _Bedside Table_, 2004. 8 x 5 inches (20.3 x 12.7 cm). Hand-bound journal, ink, watercolor. Photo by Aleia Woolsey

Naturalists write about and draw what they observe. In the days before photography, every expedition that set out to explore an unknown continent—or mountain range, or archipelago—included people whose job it was to document all the plants and animals encountered, as well as any indigenous people, structures, and other artifacts. Because the naturalist was the person who documented and communicated what the group saw. Accuracy was imperative. Amateur naturalists were no less careful as they recorded their own finds, and many of their observations also added greatly to the body of scientific information.

The naturalist sees the world as describable, catalogable, and ultimately controllable and understandable. This is very different from wabi-sabi: whereas the wabi-sabi world is always in flux, always shifting and changing, the naturalist's world is made up of creatures and objects that can be described and become, in a sense, fixed. Although typically about the natural world, a naturalist's journal can include any subject matter. If you have a naturalist's worldview, whether you're interested in unusual fungi and lichens, the ruins you encounter on a vacation in Mexico, or the intriguing variety of lawn ornaments in your neighborhood, your concern will be with getting all the details right.

This type of journal will probably be kept on plain, unadorned paper with entries done in pen or pencil with perhaps a little light watercolor wash. Rather than having extravagant embellishment, this journal will be functional, and its beauty will lie in the precision of its sketches, maps, and diagrams. A crisp descriptive text that explains and expands the entries will never overwhelm them. A naturalist takes a look around and says, "Let me describe, not judge, not get emotional about all of this. I'll put down the facts, as clearly as I can and without interpretation, and let the facts speak for themselves."

Saturday morning, before I really opened my eyes, Lake Michigan was just outside my window.

Fred planted a sunflower or two in our Zinnia bed

**Edie Greene, *Untitled Journal Page*, 2004. 8³/₄ x 6³/₄ in. (22.2 x 17.1 cm).
Hand-bound journal, computer paper, pen and ink, watercolor wash; left-handed drawing and painting. Photo by Aleia Woolsey**

Later, we saw shells like this as part of a 40,000,000 yr old fossil

We watched sea snails & hermit crabs crawling through the pond.

Shells from Ao Nang & Koh Yao Noi

Many of these shells were found in a tidal estuary where we saw mudskippers jumping b/t water & land!

Phang Nga Bay National paddling Park

MANGROVE FOREST (Day 1)

Paddling in Thailand white breasted sea eagle

Phuket

Koh Yao Noi

Hong Island (Day 2)

Koh Yao Yai

Ao Nang

Railay

Krabi

**Kerstin Vogdes, *Travel Journal: Thailand and Cambodia*,
2004. Bound journal, PVA glue, ink, shells.
Photo by Aleia Woolsey**

53

Drawing Accurately

One of the main skills that you will use in your naturalist's journal is realistic drawing, which is more about learning to see than about making art. The task of this kind of drawing is to render in two dimensions that which exists in three. The first step of this process is to choose a point of view and to maintain it throughout. Neither subject nor viewer can change positions once the drawing has begun because of the simple fact that when either you or the thing you are drawing moves, everything changes.

The main obstacle to drawing accurately is your brain, which is filled with information that will not help you: "Tabletops are rectangular," your brain whispers to you, so you draw a perfect rectangle. "The table has four legs of equal length," says your brain, so you draw them; and immediately you realize that your drawing looks like your five-year-old nephew made it. To overcome your brain, you need to measure and compare—that's all there is to it.

Let's draw just a tabletop to learn this measuring method. Look around and find a tabletop. The first step will be to pick out the four lines that make up its edges, lines A-B, B-C, C-D, D-A (see figure 1 on page 55). Choose the shortest of those four, A-B in this example, and measure it using the pencil tip and your thumb like this: imagine you are looking at the table through a glass windowpane that's an arm's length in front of you. Close one eye and look at the table, as if holding a pencil flat up

Pamela Averick, *Untitled Journal Page*, 2004. Photo by Gwen Diehn

to the glass. Keeping your elbow straight so that your eye and your pencil remain the same distance apart at all times while measuring, and always keeping the pencil flat on the glass, rotate the pencil on the glass until the line you are measuring appears to be parallel with or covered by the pencil. Place the tip of the pencil at the start of line A-B, and mark with your thumb the end of line A-B on your pencil. This measurement, from the pencil tip to your thumb, is your "unit." You'll use it to measure the other lines so they all appear on your paper in correct proportion to one another.

Holding the position of unit A-B on your pencil, see how many of them fit along line B-C. This gives you the first proportion. To transfer it to paper, start by choosing a length for line A-B. The size of this first line will determine the size of the finished drawing, so choose the size while considering how big your page is, as well as how big the

Kerstin Vogdes, *Sketches of LBI*, 2001. Bound journal, ink, watercolors. Photo by Aleia Woolsey

drawing needs to be. Draw line A-B, angling it as nearly as possible to the way it's angled in real life. Now draw line B-C, making it as many units long as it was when you measured it. Continue measuring and drawing in the same way for the other two lines of the tabletop.

Besides measuring, comparing one part to another is a very helpful device. Look at point B on the back of the tabletop. If you want to be sure you have angled line A-B correctly, imagine a line dropping straight down from point B and intersecting the front of the table, line D-A, at point E (see figure 2). How does the distance between section A-E compare in length with your original unit, A-B? If you've put point B too far over in either direction, move it to the right spot so that point B relates to line D-A correctly. Now erase your original line A-B and redraw it. This time the angle formed by line A-B and line D-A should be accurate (see figure 3). Check point C in the same way.

A third useful device is that of using horizontals and verticals to check how far off the horizontal or vertical a line should be. Hold the pencil straight up and down. Notice how far off the vertical line of the pencil the side of the table, line A-B, seems to move. Hold the pencil horizontally and use it to judge the rise or fall of the back edge. Does it rise slightly, fall slightly or remain truly horizontal? It's good to check horizontals and verticals periodically while doing a drawing.

You can use these same three techniques to draw anything. Always start by lightly sketching in the general shapes.

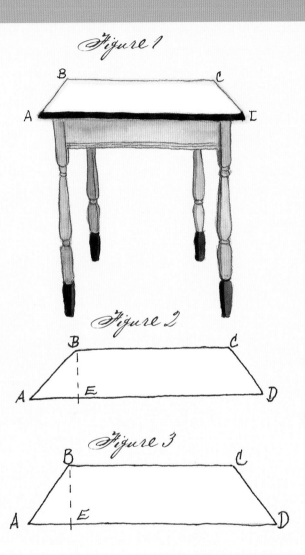

Figure 1

Figure 2

Figure 3

Once the general parts are drawn proportionately, apply the same three devices—measuring, comparing, and judging horizontals and verticals—to smaller and smaller parts. It's very important to move from the general to the particular. If you don't have the general proportions right, no matter how perfectly you've rendered tiny details, the drawing is not going to look right. You have to earn the right to draw the details.

This is a very brief introduction to drawing, but mastering these techniques will enable you to make much progress. Take these very basic drawing instructions and use them over and over. Drawing is to art as arpeggios and scales are to composing music. A drawing teacher can jump-start you and give you some hints, but the only way to really learn how to draw is to do it. And do it. And do it.

The Spiritual World

In the Medieval period in Europe (between A.D. 500 and 1450), the visible, material world was viewed as merely a prelude to the spiritual world in which souls were believed to live after earthly life was over. The artwork of the time reflected this worldview in that, rather than focusing on the muddy details of everyday life, it abounded in colors and images that expressed and aroused emotion and helped move the viewer to a more spiritual attitude. It was not concerned with describing the natural world, but used elements of the natural world as symbols that spoke to people about the world to come.

Gothic cathedrals, such as Chartres in France, are in a sense machines that work on the body—the perceptions and senses—in order to catapult the visitor or worshipper to a higher spiritual plane. The means used to achieve this transformation include light and geometry. The light comes from the expanse of stained glass that encloses and fills the interior with pure color and luminance. The geometry comes from nature.

The builders of these cathedrals understood that certain proportions and sequences of intervals occur over and over throughout the natural world. Because this geometry seemed to be the foundation of nature, it was assumed to reflect the mind of God. One of these universals is known as the Golden Proportion. The Golden Proportion is found in the human body, in the wings of birds and insects, in seashells, and in many other places. In a Golden Rectangle, which is derived from the Golden Proportion, the short side is related to the long side in the same way that the long side is related to the sum of the short side and long side (see A Golden Journal on page 58). This rectangle seems to be extraordinarily pleasing to humans as it also occurs over and over, not only in nature, but also in ancient and modern buildings and in artwork from many cultures.

In a Gothic cathedral, the proportions are frequently Golden. The hoped-for result of the light, the music (whose mathematical properties echo many of the geometrical properties of the architecture of the cathedral), and the architecture is that worshippers are emotionally transported out of their everyday lives and into a state of meditation and prayer. (This is a gross simplification of a subject that warrants greater discussion. For more information, an excellent source is Robert Lawler's *Sacred Geometry*, published in 1982 by Thames and Hudson.)

Well now, how on earth can a journal transport someone in such a way? Tim Ely is a book artist who considers some books to be akin to cathedrals in that they also can act on the body to attune it to a higher, more spiritual frequency. Ely uses some of the same means as the cathedral builders. He constructs his books so that the dimensions form Golden Rectangles. Many elements on the pages also display the Golden Proportion and Rectangle as well as other pro-

Charlotte Hedlund, *Untitled Journal Page*, 2003. 8 x 6 inches (20.3 x 15.2 cm). Bound journal, bristol board on handmade paper book page, PVA glue, acrylic paint, ink; glued and painted. Photo by artist

Jane Dalton, *La Playa*, 2004. 8 x 5 inches (20.3 x 12.7 cm). Hand-bound journal, watercolor pencils, micron pen. Photo by Aleia Woolsey

portions and geometric forms from Sacred Geometry. He lavishes enormous care and craftsmanship on the construction of his books. Often he adds a few drops of essential oil—lavender or rosemary perhaps—to the paste that he cooks to use as book adhesive. The result is a book that feels wonderful in the hand, a vibrating, auratic object that points to meanings far beyond the literal.

A spiritual-emotional journal then is one that grabs the reader by the neck and gives a tug and a shake. "Wake up!" it whispers. "Things are not what they seem to be on the surface!" This is a journal filled with rich colors and textures that invite contemplation and meditation. The book itself might be covered with velvet, soft leather, or some other material that feels good to hold. Pages may be laden with imagery, or they might consist of solid fields of colors with loose handwriting that leaps and skips and races across them. Whichever, the images and text in the journal deal with a spiritual interpretation of the world. This journal might also include reflections that draw meaning out of events and that move the journal keeper into a more spiritual realm of practice.

Even though the term *journal* itself refers to the everyday, this journal doesn't have to stay with the quotidian or mundane interpretation of things. The same events and objects that might lead a naturalist to make careful and intellectually satisfying drawings and descriptions will inspire the spiritual journalist to reflect on the broader meaning, beyond material appearances. The same flower that the naturalist draws with precision becomes a simplified, colorful form—perhaps a part of a border—in the spiritual journal, a symbol that points beyond itself to the sacred, to the ecstatic, to the spiritual.

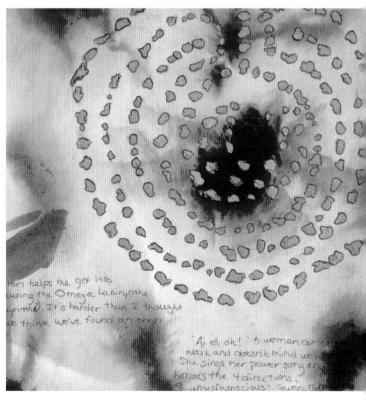

Janet Scholl, *Untitled Journal Page*, 2004. Text-weight paper, liquid acrylics, pen. Photo by Gwen Diehn.

A Golden Journal

f you would like to make your own spiritual journal, try using a Golden Rectangle for the overall shape. To construct this rectangle, first draw a square with its side the same length that you want the shorter dimension of the book's cover to be (see figure 1).

Now put a dot at the midpoint of sides AB and CD, and join the midpoints (see figure 2). Use a ruler to extend lines AB and CD, as in figure 3.

Now put one point of a compass (you can also use a piece of string pulled taut) at point E and the point of the compass pencil at point D (if using string, simply hold one end down at point E and, keeping it taut, hold the other end of the string with two fingers where it touches point D), as shown in figure 4. Then draw the arc to DG, which will intersect the extension of line AB at point G. (If using string, keep holding the measured length of string, one finger pressing it down at point D, and swing it to find out where it crosses the extension of AB, which is where you will make a mark, at G.)

Use a triangle to draw a straight line up from point G to a point H on the extension of line CD. The rectangle ACHG is a Golden Rectangle. Line AC is to line AG as line AG is to the sum of CA and AG.

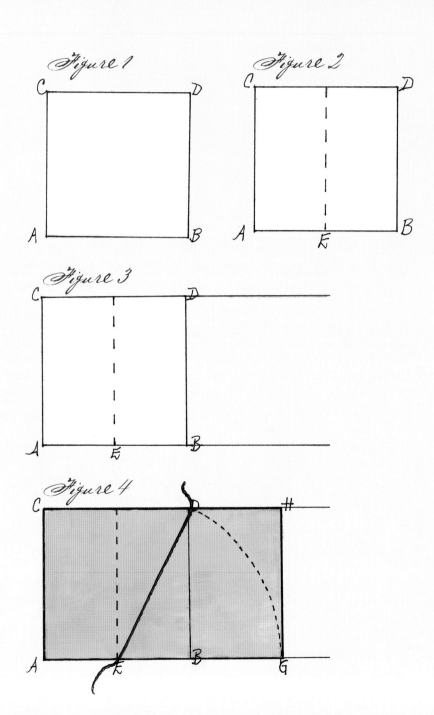

The Symbolic World

In Australian Aboriginal culture, the material world, and particularly the landscape, is a giant mnemonic device, a memory aid at the service of helping people remember the stories of their culture. A group of people walking across the dessert might stop at a gently sloping hill with several large boulders strewn along the ridge and there, prompted by the extremely subtle configuration of the land, sing a story about one of their ancestors. In this way the people have kept both their land and their stories alive.

In a custom completely alien to us in the west (who happily bulldoze grassy hillsides in order to flatten the land for the cheaper construction of tanning salons and gas stations, mini malls and karate parlors), Aborigines traditionally make annual walking journeys along ancient paths that they call "songlines." The stories they sing as they walk tell the history of their ancestors and of the time they call the Dreaming. For them, the material world is symbolic of a greater reality.

There are symbolic elements in our world, too. Places as well as objects that have been the scene of the events of our lives can become laden with associations. Frequently used objects sometimes seem to carry an aura of the person who used them. My grandfather's fountain pen rests on a shelf in my studio, and it never fails to remind me of the fact that he gave me my own first pen when I was in third grade—a maroon colored Esterbrook that my teacher confiscated, telling me I was too young to write with a pen!

A journal can be used to record and reflect on these symbols. Dream journals, especially, fall into the category of symbolic journals because the images in dreams are themselves symbols. Years ago I saw a beautiful, evocative dream journal in an exhibition of artwork by members of a society dedicated to the study of dreams. The little book was a journey through the nighttime landscape of the artist's dreams, and the symbols became a language that gave her a fine tool for interpretation.

The keeper of a symbolic journal will seek out patterns and motifs that summarize places, people, and ideas as well as dreams. Instead of making a realistic drawing of a landscape, this journaler is more likely to use the colors in the landscape in abstract shapes that float behind or beside text. A border of repeating abstract forms might hint at the season or the amount and kind of vegetation. When traveling, this kind of journaler might make rubbings of textures found in a place or simplify the forms of indigenous housing in the area visited.

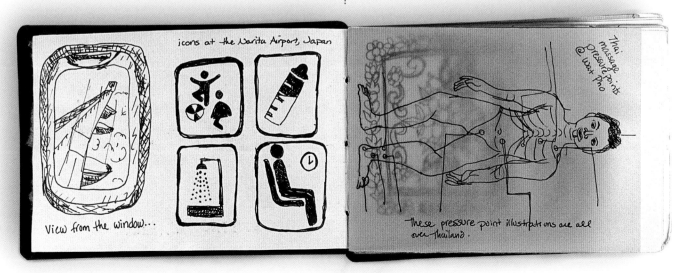

Kerstin Vogdes, *Travel Journal: Thailand and Cambodia*, 2004. 4 x 6 inches (10.2 x 15.2 cm) Hand-bound journal, PVA glue, vellum, ink, shells. Photo by Aleia Woolsey

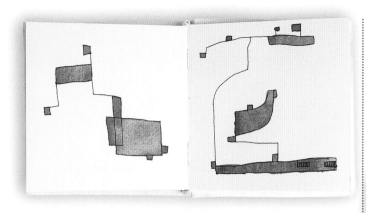

Val Lucas, *Untitled page from July*, 2004 journal. 4 x 4 inches,
(10.2 x 10.2 cm), watercolor, pen, hand-bound journal

Some symbolic journals have no text. The entire record is
made in images, which are densely packed symbols. Let's
say I have a complicated dream about driving a car that
loses power slowly and can't move fast enough. Although
many things happen in the dream (and many events are
so fragmentary and ephemeral that I can't remember
them clearly, nor put them into words), the feeling of
being in a powerless car stays with me. My symbol for
this dream might be my car with a large boulder tied to
the back bumper, attempting to climb a hill.

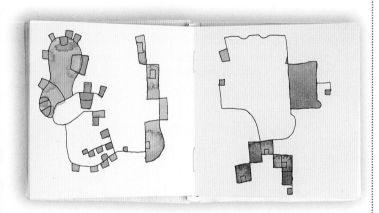

Val Lucas, *Untitled page from July*, 2004 journal. 4 x 4 inches,
(10.2 x 10.2 cm), watercolor, pen, hand-bound journal

**Each page in Val's journal symbolically records her journey through
life that day.**

Kelcey Loomer, *Untitled Journal Page*, 2001. 11 x 8¹/₄ inches
(27.9 x 21 cm). acrylic paint, ink pen. Photo by Aleia Woolsey

Other symbolic journals may be filled with text, the
words themselves sketching metaphors and symbols for
experiences that defy being pinned down and put into
literal form. An important medium for symbolic jour-
nalers is collage of appropriated imagery. In using
appropriated imagery, we harvest images as well as text
from other sources and use these fragments as marks in
a new, original expression. Collaged elements always
carry some meaning and connotation from their former
lives, and in this way they become symbolic. A piece of
ephemera from everyday life—a theater ticket perhaps—
will not only have the literal meaning "ticket stub," but
will also carry some meaning based on its original context: "Romeo and Juliet" performed at the Folger
Shakespeare Theatre or "Spiderman 2" playing at a
multi-plex theater outside of Toledo, Ohio. A piece of
paper with a print of a drawing or painting will obvi-
ously bring meaning, but also a scrap of patterned wrapping paper will be a reminder of a certain gift, and as
such will carry connotative meaning beyond the pretty,
if commonplace, pattern printed on it.

Making the Invisible Visible

The bringing of one's past, present, emotions, hopes, fears, fleeting interests, prejudices, and any other contexts to the act of drawing enlivens it in a way that pure objective copying of nature never can. All the possible ways of seeing and of experiencing a place are crucial to the various possibilities for representing it. For this reason I love drawing the same scene over and over at different times in my life. I also love looking at 20 different people's interpretation of the same scene.

It's true that sometimes we draw to fix something in our minds or to learn more about it. (Today I drew a map of my house and yard so I could remember which bushes the tree man will remove when he comes to do some major yard work in a couple of weeks.) But it's also true that we draw to give visible form to that which can't be seen—to give form to evening breezes, creepy feelings, and unearthly coincidences. Drawing in many different ways—sometimes tight renderings, sometimes the barest minimum of fat lines, sometimes a spattering of color, sometimes a fretful hatching of lines—allows us to not only reproduce what we can see but also to make the invisible visible for ourselves as well as to anyone else who might look at our work.

Years ago, the painter Jennifer Bartlett rented a villa in the south of France for several months. Her dream of working in a beautiful place with balmy weather came crashing down around her ears when the place itself turned out to be ugly and the weather even worse. After days and days of cold rain and wind, after star-

Jennifer Bartlett, *In the Garden, #51*. Photo copyright Jennifer Bartlette

ing out of her windows into a mediocre little garden-with its indifferent pool and trite little garden statue, its row of tedious trees, its uninspiring shrubbery—Bartlett decided to not only accept the circumstances in which she found herself, but to use them as the foundation of an experiment that would test the parameters of an artistic problem.

Bartlett went out and bought a large supply ofpaper and an assortment of materials: pencils, pens, charcoal, paints. She began setting up a journal-like situation in that she ruled off two rectangles on each of the first several dozen pieces of paper. The pile of neatly ruled paper was in a very real sense a blank (if unbound) journal. Her assignment to herself was to draw what she could see out of her window, and to

draw it again, and again, and again, and again until she had used up all of the paper. She began drawing on an afternoon in January and completed the project some 15 months later with nearly 200 completed drawings—all of the same patch of garden.

Bartlett did the first drawings from life, getting down as much as possible of exactly what she could see. She began with pencil, moved to colored pencil, and then back to pencil. These first drawings are similar to each other in composition and in their inclusion of details, varied surface renderings, and in Bartlett's apparent attempts to create three-dimensional space. She then moved to pen and ink, and the drawings became more simplified and veered toward the abstract. She varied the focus: in one drawing the trees are prominent, in another the pool and statue dominate and seem to stand on end, in another the entire scene is reduced to a series of dashes and dots. Periodically she returned to a more naturalistic rendering, but here also the focus and point of view changed from drawing to drawing.

By drawing number 15, the drawings, although still grounded in the pool, statue, trees, shrubbery, and grass, seem to be more about Bartlett's response to the scene than about literal rendering. Some drawings have a brooding quality. Others seem light-hearted and playful. When she begins to use watercolor, outlines melt and the drawings become even more abstract. There are drawings that focus tightly on the water in the pool and the way light plays on the surface. There are others that take a high point of view and reduce the pool to a tiny feature in what looks like a huge expanse of space. Some drawings explode out of their borders, with the trees behind the pool shooting up like flames.

When Bartlett returns to pencil after a number of color drawings, the drawings return to a more literal, naturalistic type, but there is a new looseness to them. Portions are left unfinished in some; another is rendered as meticulously as an architect's drawing, but the trees behind the pool dissolve into squiggles and melt into the sky. Pen and wash drawings become bolder and simpler as the series progresses; watercolor drawings dissolve into dots or pale washes with barely any reference to the scene. And always, after a number of abstract drawings, there is a coming back to the naturalistic, which seems a sort of summing up of new things experienced or learned.

About a quarter of the way through the series, the drawings get bigger, and each one takes up its own sheet of paper. Then suddenly a tiny set of two drawings appears, looking like something seen through the wrong end of a telescope, with a fat white border framing the drawings. Later, the drawings return to the original two-to-a-page format.

The enormous variety of these drawings points to the enormous variety of the garden itself when one stops imposing expectations on it and begins to experience it as a new place every day. What Bartlett has done is to bring her constantly changing emotions, memories, stories, and interests to this place, and allow her drawings to be guided by her daily varying purposes and intents. And this is where, to me, her work has great interest to any journal keeper. Her work highlights the fact that what we do in our journals is as much a part of who we are as what we see and experience. It doesn't matter if "nothing ever happens to me" or "I live in a boring place."

Bartlett's complete series has been dispersed, but a record of it still exists in book form. Search used bookstores and libraries for *In the Garden* by Jennifer Bartlett with an introduction by John Russell, published in 1982 by Harry N. Abrams, Inc., New York.

BURANO

Faith McLellan, *Lunch on Burano*, 2004. Bound journal, gluestick, watercolor, pencil, rubber stamp, pen, candy wrapper ephemera; painted, drawn, glued, stamped. Photo by artist

The Inner World

The Inner World

**Andrea A. Peterson, *Ox Bow*, 2003. 12 x 18 inches (30.5 x 45.7 cm).
Coptic hand-bound journal, cotton rag handmade paper, tracing paper,
colored pencil, charcoal, pastel; drawn and glued. Photo by artist**

When my friend Bette begins a new drawing, she makes random marks on a piece of paper, back and forth, up and down—soft sweeps of her pencil, marks made with no conscious intention. Inevitably, after a while, an image begins to emerge. For Bette, the image is often a face, but sometimes animals or objects appear. Only then does Bette begin to work consciously on the drawing. She believes that by restraining her conscious mind at first, she allows images to well up from her subconscious.

Bette's manner of working is related to ideas developed by a group of artists and writers in the early 20th century called the Surrealists. The Surrealists were influenced by the then-new practice of psychoanalysis, in which the patients' unconscious or subconscious minds were revealed by means of certain techniques. The intended result was to free the patients from the hold these hidden parts of the psyche had on their lives.

The Surrealists invented games and practices aimed at releasing subconscious imagery. One of their practices was what they called automatic writing—writing that was done spontaneously with no thought and with no effort at making rational sense or even recognizable meaning. Games, too, with names such as "The Exquisite Corpse," involved random acts of writing that were believed to generate true creative results. Dream imagery was very important to them because it emerged from the unconscious mind.

A recent practice designed to get around the censoring intellect (which can so easily freeze us in our efforts to come up with new ideas) is Julia Cameron's Morning Pages exercise. Cameron has designed a program to free the artist she believes to be within each person. One of the core practices of her program is to bounce out of bed in the morning and immediately write three pages in a journal. If nothing comes, it's okay to write something along the lines of, "I have nothing to write today," over and over again to fill the pages. Once the pages are complete, they are put away unread until much later. Cameron believes that morning pages tap into our unconscious minds in a way that can't be done later in the day after we're fully awake and functioning.

If a naturalist's journal is focused on the world outside of us, the inner journal is the polar opposite. An inner journal is about me: the writer and artist. The visuals in the journal may grow out of doodles and random marks, or they may be fragments of images that we've come across and that have somehow beckoned to us, like shiny objects calling to a crow. Poured paint might suggest an image that the journal keeper will coax out of the random shapes on the page. Words overheard in a restaurant might spark associations that lead to revelations. This is the journal in which to explore just what it is that your eye loves to look at, and also just

Kelcey Loomer, *Untitled Journal Page*, 2004. 9¹/₄ x 6¹/₄ inches (23.5 x 15.9 cm).
Pen, pencil, oil pastel, watercolor, ribbon. Photo by Aleia Woolsey

why it is that your eye loves to look at that particular image. It is a place to express your thoughts and feelings about the sounds your ear loves to hear.

This is the journal to angrily fling paint at without understanding quite why, and then to come back to later and refine the shapes that seems to peek out from behind the colors. Lists of words, collections of sounds, pieces of ephemera, and patches of texture—all of these can be held safe in this journal, percolating, until someday, years later, you return to this old book and find yourself able to see patterns and ideas and images you never suspected at the time.

This is also the journal for whining about relationships, and fretting about your children, and getting excited about new discoveries, and explaining your feelings in more detail than any of your friends would have the patience to listen to. This journal is the grown-up sister of the diary I kept in high school, the one in which I carried on for 12 pages trying to decide exactly what it was that so-and-so-meant when he said thus and so, and not only that, but—12 more pages—how would I possibly live without him, and moreover, he certainly wasn't worth all this agony, so there!

Julie Wagner, *Insomniac's Journal*, 2001. 9¹/₄ x 8³/₄ x 1 inches (23.5 x 22.2 x 2.5 cm).
Stab bound journal, mulberry paper, ink, oil-transfer drawing. Photo by Dan Morse

Victoria Rabinowe, *Dream Journal Drawings*, 2004.
8¹/₄ x 7 x ¹/₂ inches (21 x 17.8 x 1.3 cm). Text woven paper, hand-drawn graphite images, pen, watercolor,
pastel; concertina structure, scanned, manipulated, computer printed. Photo by artist

The Power of Words

by Ann Turkle

I asked my friend Ann Turkle, a long-time writer and visual journaler, to write a few words about the ongoing relationship between the verbal and visual in journaling. You'll find the prompts she provides are one way to begin accessing your inner world through words.

Ann Turkle, *Ireland Journal*, 2004. 3 x 3¹/₂ inches (7.6 x 14 cm). Hand-bound, pen and watercolor. Photo by Aleia Woolsey

f I pick up an illustrated journal and leaf through it, the visual images immediately compel my attention. As someone who works more often in words, I'm a little jealous of the power of pictures. Fortunately this is not an either/or proposition. The satisfactions that develop as you engage in journal keeping are richer when they involve both the visual and the verbal. The journal filled with visual images and verbal observations offers a field of play where you can exercise for years to come. And hindsight, in the case of looking back on your journals, may be instructive and rewarding.

STRETCH YOUR WRITING MUSCLES

In the theatre, the person who rescues actors who forget their lines is the prompter, and as writers, it's useful to have prompts to help us begin laying down some lines in our journals. At the end of this section is a series of short prompts. One of the tricks to using prompts is to let them tickle a latent urge on your part. If you are a lover of words, the prompt's encouragement to "steal language," to take down words and figures of speech as you hear them during the day, may allow the journal to be in your thoughts, even if you don't have it with you. As a child, I often filled the margins of my homework papers with my initials, trying for a distinctive monogram. You can still play with lettering or alter your handwriting; and freeing the forms of the letters may loosen the content of your writing as well.

Jot down an appreciation of what this day has offered you while you sit at a stoplight or wait for your e-mail connection to come on-line, and you will produce journal fodder as well as improve the complexion of your day. Take a pen and 3 x 5-inch (7.6 x12.7 cm) cards with you wherever you go, and even the smallest pauses become an opportunity to take down a few words or an image. Don't worry if you are not sure you understand a prompt. Do with it whatever you want. There will be no final exams.

When confronted with a journal, some of us have a flashback to the guilt associated with failed diaries and the daunting memory of blank pages stretching into the months and years. And what I managed to get onto those diary pages often resembled what I like to call a "brain in a jar," a collection of thoughts and feelings devoid of any setting in time place or circumstance. The texture of what you witness, what you see and hear and smell, should make its way into your writing. Sit down for 10 minutes and simply record everything you notice-the ticking of the clock, the hum of the dehumidifier, the smell of the damp earth outside your door, the grinding gears of the garbage truck on the street, the green light reflecting off the rhododendron leaves into your study. Native American author N. Scott Momoday observes, "The events of one's life take place, *take place*." We require a setting. Let the life around you come onto the pages of your journal.

Another trick to using prompts well is to work in a series. This saves you from making a decision each time you find a few minutes to write, and it provides you an opportunity to observe patterns. Pick an easily accessible place and visit it several times a week. Observe changes and the subtle shift from season to season. Detail the progress of your garden. Keep track of your child or spouse in some small but telling way. The life you save in a journal will most definitely be your own.

PULL TOGETHER

Several of the prompts suggest opportunities to overlap writing and drawing. If you do a room journal, your office can come alive on the page as you observe it in sketches and words. The common objects on a nightstand, drawn and labeled, take on personality and remind you of a specific point in time. When reaching for inspiration, we often ignore what's right under our noses. Draw the kitchen counter with its ingredients for the eggplant casserole; write out the recipe.

DIVE BACK IN

Many journal keepers save their journals, but too often they use them only to revisit an earlier experience. The journals we have kept can provide a fresh means of knowing ourselves. Welsh artist Timothy Emlyn Jones tells of an encounter with psychologist Marion Milner, who, under the pen name of Joanna Field, wrote influential books about the individual's encounter with creativity. As Milner and Jones explored the question of how he chose the subject matter for his art, Milner mirrored back to him his process as "choosing what his eye

Ann Turkle, *Ireland Journal*, 2004. Photo by Aleia Woolsey

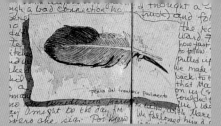

Gwen Diehn, Details of *Untitled Journal Page*. 6 x 9 inches
(15.2 x 22.9 cm). Pen and watercolor on handmade paper. Photo by Aleia Woolsey

liked." As Jones explored this notion, he discovered he should "surrender to his subject." And as he wrote about his process, he found language could help him "draw out his drawings." Our own work can become the object of very productive research.

What can your journals tell you about what your eye likes? And having discovered that, why not stay with that particular subject for a while? A student, Rena Kaneko, spent three years exploring in several different art forms a photograph of her mother's sister, who had died as an infant. She drew the image, carved a woodblock of it, made an artists' book using the image, and wrote about it in her poetry and essays.

In a reflection on her process of pursuing this image over three years, Rena said, "Both writing and visual art helped me to understand the significant terms by which I define myself. . . by showing me my vision. I saw my own memory seeping through my words and imagery. They are the memories that remained with me, the memories I unconsciously made a decision to let stay, that seemed to sculpt my identity. Whether I was making a print of my aunt or writing about the image, I was also journeying deeply into the history of my self-formation. Through a creative process, I saw the sequences of remembered images that reminded me vividly of who I am." (Rena Kaneko; unpublished thesis; Warren Wilson College, 2004)

There are four prompts near the end of the list that allow you to get reacquainted with journals you have kept. Perhaps you will come upon images that will reward your patience and tenacity by allowing you to see more clearly who you are and fill you with energy to continue your efforts. One of the most useful lessons contained in your journals is the truth that you will learn as much from your own work as you will from any teacher.

PROMPTS

1. Divide a page into nine squares. Practice seeing accurately with words and drawings.

2. Choose a plot of land. Visit it daily. Capture its changes.

3. Use your non-dominant hand to write the answer to a difficult question.

4. Fill a page with words. Allow no white space.

5. Use a single image, written or drawn. Repeat its pattern.

6. Write your life story in 250 words, exactly.

7. Write your life story using a single subject: my life in cars (an "auto" biography?), my life in shoes, my life in food, my life in movies.

8. Steal language. Take down words you hear, figures of speech, bits of conversation.

9. Learn new words. Develop dictionary pages. Create your own definitions.

10. Make lists of what you like—poetry, movies, people, stories, art, songs. Why do you like these things?

11. Make lists.

12. Write a history of your body. Illustrate it.

13. Make a list of everything you notice while sitting in one place.

14. Devote several pages in the journal to rooms. Draw and write about your living space.

15. Draw and write about a countertop, a medicine chest, a nightstand.

16. Let others write in your journal.

17. Appreciate the gifts of the day.

18. Vary your layout. For one day, change your ratio of visuals and words.

19. Capture a "found poem" from everyday language, headlines, or street signs.

20. Change your handwriting or letterforms. If you write, then print. Use only upper or lower case letters.

21. Reread your journal as if it were fiction. What's the story?

22. Write an acknowledgments page for your journal. Who has helped you in this effort?

23. Reread your journal. Create a table of contents or an index.

24. Reread your journal. Write a preface. Write its epilogue.

25. Write 10 more prompts.

Pages in Stages: Ways of Working

Whether you're interested in working in many overlapping layers or in composing clear, concise pages with a minimum of visual noise, it's useful to work in stages. A visual journal, at its most simple, is an interplay between text and image that conveys meaning. However, if you take this too seriously, you can build a certain amount of anxiety over facing the blank page—and this is the exact opposite feeling you want to bring to your work. It might help you to think in terms of beginning processes (starters), middle processes (middles), and final processes (toppings). Working this way can give you enough of a structure to start your practices flowing. When you work in stages, you'll find your pages will pull together in a whole new way.

In this chapter, you'll find ideas for carrying your pages to completion. Working in stages is a mix-and-match exercise with no right or wrong answers. You can combine starters, middles, and toppers any way you please. Write or draw on a map, use metallic pens for text in a collage, flow a watercolor wash over writing, use an opaque ground to "erase" your work and start again, make your own stamps to create a border, remove pages or laminate them—the combinations are endless.

Clare Duplace,
Untitled Journal Page, 2004.
Ink, feather pen, foil, gouache, hairpins.
Photo by Aleia Woolsey

Starters, Bases, and Other Ways of Beginning

Where to begin? Ideas you want to convey and feelings you want to portray and evoke are bubbling inside you. The choices seem limitless, if not daunting, when you're facing a new page. The ideas presented here will give you a nudge to get you started.

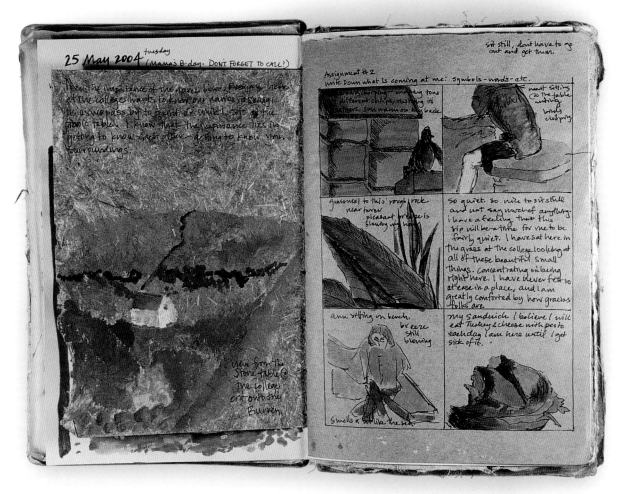

Sarah A. Bourne, *Ireland Journal Page,* **2004. 8¹/₂ x 11 inches (21.6 x 27.9 cm).**
Bound journal, handmade paper, drawing paper, watercolor, ink. Photo by Aleia Woolsey

PAPER

When you begin to incorporate images into a journal, suddenly the very paper on which you're working takes on new importance and actually becomes the first stage. It's a great boon if the paper is sufficiently alluring to make you look forward to putting down some marks. If it provides you, the journal keeper, with the impetus to work, an interesting paper may be all the starter that you need.

In a very real way, the paper itself is a part of every image, in some cases forming a ground that reflects its own whiteness and adds sparkle and light to the drawn or painted images. In other instances the paper acts as a foil or counterpoint to the work that is done on it, thus creating a nice tension and edginess. Sometimes the paper provides a wash of color, an emotional tone, or a sense of the past. Sometimes the paper lends a sense of order or control.

You may be lucky enough to find enticing paper already bound in a journal that you fall in love with. Its heavy pages with just a hint of a creamy peachy color invite your pen to stroke them. You love the shape and size of the pages—best of all, the book fits perfectly in your coat pocket. But even if you can't find a journal that you love, you can usually find paper that you love, and you can easily make a journal out of this paper (see The Reluctant Bookbinder, pages 99 to 114) or modify a blank book to include this paper (see Customizing a Blank Book on page 116).

POURED COLORS

Sometimes beautiful paper isn't sufficient to get you going. If you need more of an invitation, try pouring colors or tints on the paper. The random patterns that result can make whatever you put on top of them more interesting. The shapes, moreover, can be the basis for a layout or page design that you would have never thought of on your own. The only caveat is that the paper needs to be substantial enough to handle getting wet. Thin, inexpensive paper wrinkles badly, and unless that's the look you want to achieve, you might want to reserve this technique for heavier pieces of paper (which you can add to a purchased journal if it has thin paper). If you're binding your own journal, simply pour the pages before cutting or tearing them and binding the book.

To pour the color, you'll need fluid acrylic paints or acrylic inks in a few colors that suit your mood for the journal. You can also use strong tea or coffee. Metallic or iridescent colors make a nice addition if you like to work on pages that sparkle or glow. Gather together a couple of old plastic squeeze bottles such as dish detergent bottles, some blotting paper or old newspaper, a piece of plastic, such as a drop cloth or a large plastic garbage bag, and water.

Begin by spreading the plastic on the floor or a tabletop, and lay a sheet of watercolor or other slightly heavy to heavy paper on it. There are several brands of text or cover paper that are wonderful choices for this process, but other multimedia papers work well, too. Pour 1 to 3 inches (2.5 to 7.6 cm) of

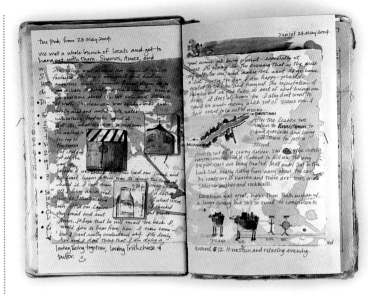

Sarah A. Bourne, *Ireland Journal Page*, 2004. 8¹/₂ x 11 inches (21.6 x 27.9 cm). Hand-bound journal, handmade paper, watercolor, ink. Photo by Aleia Woolsey

water in each bottle, then add a couple of drops of paint or ink, and shake the bottle to mix. If the colors seem too dark and heavy, add more water. If the colors are too light or thin, add more paint. If you're using tea or coffee, there's no need to dilute.

Materials for pouring color onto a page

Gwen Diehn, *Untitled Journal Page*. 6 x 9 inches (15.2 x 22.9 cm). Watercolor on handmade paper page with poured fluid acylic. Photo by Aleia Woolsey

Now simply squirt or dribble the watery paint onto the paper. You can:

- move the paint around on the page by rolling the paper or by gently folding (but not creasing) each corner into the center and then back out

- press another piece of the same kind of paper on top of the first sheet, thereby making two sheets at once

- blot the color to lighten it

- add layers of color, letting colors dry between layers

- hold it up so that rivers of color trickle down toward the edges

- spread the paint with your hands or a sponge or a brush

- do anything else that makes the kind of marks you want to make.

When you're finished with one side, turn the page over and do the other side. Hang the sheet up on a clothesline to dry or drape it over the back of a chair or a drying rack. After it dries, the paper will look even more spectacular. You can then cut or tear it down to the size you need it to be. You can't go wrong with this process!

As mentioned, you can do the same process using watercolors, strong coffee or tea, or water-based inks. However, these media can be rewet, and painting over them with more water media will move the dye or pigment around and change the shapes they form on the paper. Because acrylics dry to a permanent state and can't be rewet, they'll remain in the shapes they were when they dried, even when you paint over them with water media. If you want to modify the hues or colors of acrylic poured paint, overlay them with thin washes of watercolor, fluid acrylics, or transparent inks.

Mary Ann Moss, *Untitled Journal Page*, 2004. 8 x 6 inches (20.3 x 15.2 cm). Handmade journal, gesso, acrylic paint, ink, water-color markers, ephemera, magazine and newspaper scraps, packing tape; glued, collaged, painted, and illustrated. Photo by artist

PRINTED FORMS

Another interesting way to get started is to use printed forms for your journal paper. Grid paper or quadrille paper, lined paper, ledger sheets, and other pre-printed forms impose order on information. Their very orderliness and fussiness invite your comments, your splashes of color, and your out-of-the-lines drawing. See what happens when you disregard the prescribed spaces and draw, paint, and write wherever you want. The order is still there, in the background, on a bottom layer, and it forms a stage on which emotion and impetuous expression are heightened by the contrast.

Search office supply stores, antique stores, and school supply stores for forms. If the paper is too flimsy for heavy, wet media, you can either laminate it to heavier paper (see Laminating Pages on page 117), or use colored pencils, pens, crayons, pencils, or light watercolor sketching when you work on those pages. An interesting example of the use of this starter is in Patterns Lost and Found (see page 80), in which the journal keeper began with pre-printed forms made specifically for recording the results of a day's fishing.

MAPS AND DIAGRAMS

Maps and other kinds of diagrams impose a different kind of order on a page. Unlike forms, these carry some content and meaning themselves and are not simply blank matrices for organizing content. They also carry connotative meaning that can enhance or act as a foil against the content you add.

There are several ways to turn a map or diagram into a first stage for a journal page. One way is to use a computer to scan the map or diagram and then print it on the paper you want to use in your journal. This method offers the most flexibility in that you can modify the color, the darkness or lightness of the print, as well as its size.

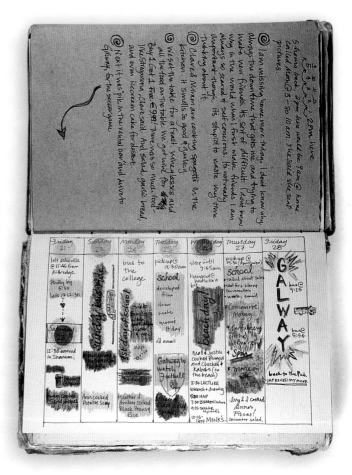

Sarah A. Bourne, *Ireland Journal Page*, 2004. 8¹/₂ x 11 inches (21.6 x 27.9 cm). Hand-bound journal, handmade paper, watercolor, ink. Photo by Aleia Woolsey

I started with a map that I had transferred onto the page before I made the journal.

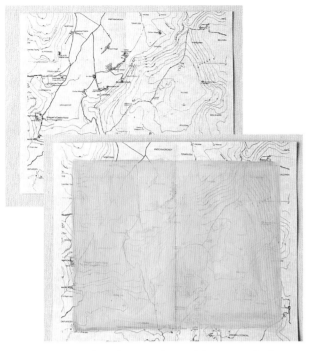

I painted out the central part of the map with white gouache to which I had added a little bit of blue watercolor.

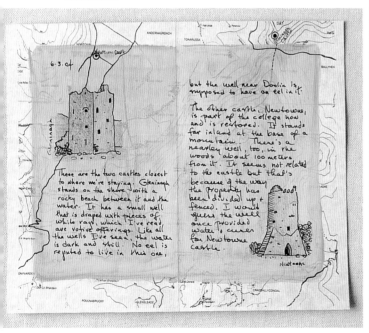

I drew and wrote, then later added watercolor to the drawing.

Gwen Diehn, *Untitled Journal Page*. 6 x 9 inches (15.2 x 22.9 cm). Watercolor, gouache, and pen over a copier transfer map. Photo by Aleia Woolsey

Another way is to glue or bind the actual map or diagram into the book. While this is the most authentic use of the item, the paper it's printed on may not be the best for the medium you'll be using on top of it. If the paper is slick and non-porous, use waterproof pens and inks, gel pens, permanent markers, and acrylic paints on it. A process that helps when painting on slick paper is to mix watercolor with a little soap or dish detergent. The soap helps break the surface tension of the water so that it adheres better to the non-porous paper.

COPIER TRANSFER

Another starter process is to make a copier transfer. This is done by making a color or black-and-white photocopy of an image, enlarging or reducing it as needed, and then brushing gel style citrus-based paint stripper on the back of the copy and burnishing with a wooden spoon to transfer the map or diagram to the paper in the journal. Fresh new photocopies work better than old ones. As shown in the photo on page 75, begin by laying the copy facedown on the journal page. To keep it from moving, you might want to tape it lightly to the page with drafting tape. Then generously brush the back of the copy with citrus-based gel-style paint stripper. Wait about 30 seconds for the gel to penetrate the paper, and then rub or burnish the back of the page with the rounded bowl of a wooden or metal spoon. Be very careful not to shift the copy as you burnish.

You can see how well the image is transferring by holding the copy in place and carefully lifting one corner at a time. If the transfer isn't dark enough, either burnish some more while applying more pressure or apply more gel before continuing to burnish. If you're still having trouble transferring the image, it may be the age of the gel stripper. If you're using stripper that's been in your workshop awhile, purchase a new container of fresh stripper.

Once the copy is transferred, you can draw or paint right on top of it, add color, and otherwise alter the image to suit your purposes. Copier transfers are a good way to introduce appropriated imagery to your work.

Kelcey Loomer, *Untitled Journal Page*, **2004. 5 x 4 inches (12.7 x 10.2 cm). Copier transfer, watercolor. Photo by Aleia Woolsey**

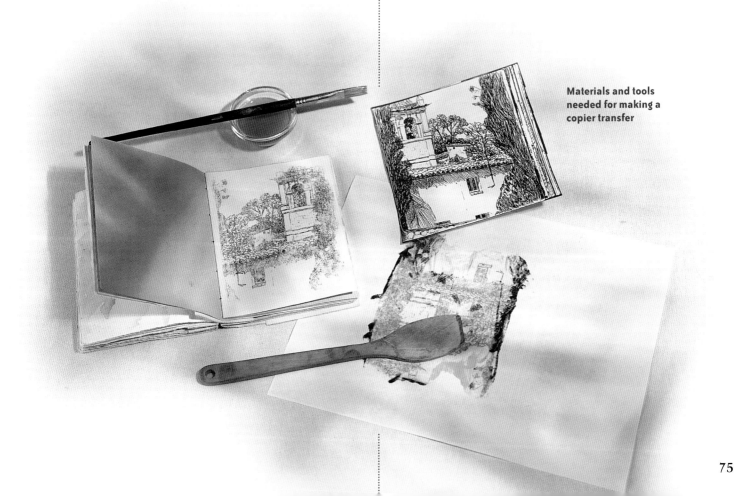

Materials and tools needed for making a copier transfer

COLLAGE

At the heart of many journals today are the scraps, the ephemera of a journey, of an experience, of a project, or of daily life. These are logical starters for use as the base of a page, or as the point of departure for drawings. Collage is equally effective as a starter, a top layer of a layered page, or as a stand-alone, simpler page. Using collage as a starter sets a context for the page that is derived from the meaning of the collaged item or items. Placing an item in the background will quietly set a tone for whatever work you put on top. If you highlight the collaged item, it can be the base for the whole page.

Some flat items to collect are photographs, computer printouts of scanned drawings and photographs, tickets, receipts, notes, napkin sketches, wrapping paper, scraps of handwriting, sugar packets, maps, seed packages, labels, magazine and newspaper clippings, pressed flowers, stamps, paper bags, and fortune-cookie fortunes.

You want to attach these objects to the page using an adhesive that's appropriate to the supporting paper as well as to the collage items (see Adhesives on

Scott Gordon, *Untitled Journal Page*, 2004. 14 x 21½ inches (35.6 x 54.6 cm). Bound journal, acrylic paint, found paper; collage. Photo by Rick Wells

page 30). Consider tearing or cutting objects into strips or small pieces as well as using the whole item. Keep in mind that the supporting paper should ideally be as heavy or heavier than the collage items. Also, if you want your journal pages to lie flat, avoid attaching large collage items that are made of a different kind of paper than the supporting page. When you adhere a piece of grained paper (and all machine-made paper is grained) to another paper, the grain pulls against the support as it dries. If the support has no grain (handmade paper) or a weak grain (light, thin machine-made paper), the result is going to be warping and curling. You can, to some degree, counteract the warping by laminating a sheet of comparable paper to the back of the collaged journal page. Doing this will equalize the pull of the grain from the heavy collage.

Keep in mind that heavily collaged pages

Collage materials

fatten the fore edge of a book. You will need to compensate for this by removing a page or two immediately in front of the collage (see Removing Pages on page 114). If some items are too bulky to attach to the book itself, make scans or photocopies of them, and attach or transfer the copy to the journal instead of using the original object. Pressed leaves and flower petals can be preserved and protected by brushing them with matte or satin finish polymer varnish. The varnish glues the flattened organic material to the page and seals out air and moisture.

Like copier transfers, collage makes use of appropriated images and words. These will bring their own accumulated meanings and connotations with them into their new configurations on your pages. These items are marks, and as such should contribute to the overall meaning of the work and not dominate the piece. Work that is basically an enshrinement of an appropriated image fails on many levels.

Manufactured images, specially packaged for collage, are a poor substitute for authentic ephemera and do nothing to further the art or the progress of the artist. You can save a lot of money by walking right past the aisle that sells packages labeled "Nostalgia" and "Beauty" and "Cute Animals," just as you avoid paint-by-numbers and coloring books when you want to engage in authentic expression. Remember that less is more.

**Kristin A. Livelsberger, *Rest*, 2003. 10 x 10 x 2³/₄ inches (25.4 x 25.4 x 7 cm).
Spiral bound journal, mounting paste, acrylic paint, found paper and paper scraps, paint swatches, pen, charcoal, tape; painted, layered, glued, and taped. Photo by Fine Art Photo Portrait Studio**

Stitching

A sometimes-overlooked way of making marks is stitching. Stitched lines lend not only color but also texture to the page. A stitched border is a tactile as well as a visual element. Depending on the expressive content of the page, you might consider using brightly colored silk threads, glittering metallics, or stark, crisp black. Stitching can also be used very effectively to attach collage elements to a page and also to attach foldouts, small booklets, and envelopes to page stubs.

CHALLENGE YOURSELF

Another type of starter comes from setting up a challenge or assignment. My friend Dana gave herself the assignment of doing a small visual journal entry every day for a year. She didn't want to do a whole page a day; rather, she drew a series of boxes on the pages of a large sketchbook. She drew small boxes, less daunting than an entire page. Each page held around 14 boxes—two weeks worth of entries. Dana began at the top lefthand corner of the first page, filling in a box a day. The challenge was to summarize the day in one succinct drawing or painting, with or without text. Dana noticed that six months into the project her entries were sometimes spilling out of their boxes. Then the boxes themselves broke ranks, as it were, and she found herself penciling in various sizes and proportions of rectangles, and the pages really began to take off!

Recently while traveling in Ireland, I decided to keep track of the dark and daylight while I was there. It would be a record of the midsummer season in this relatively northern place. I made a small journal with a 3 x 3-inch (7.6 x 7.6 cm) cover and 21 pages, one for each day that I was to be there. Using a piece of rubber-stamp material, I carved a stamp that printed a scale of small lines and numbers showing midnight, 6 a.m., noon, and 6 p.m. I printed the scale at the bottom of each page. On each page I then recorded the dark and daylight hours by coloring in the scale to correspond to the light and dark. I also recorded sunrise and sunset, the phase of the moon, the weather, and, eventually, events from each day. The finished journal shows graphically the gradual shrinking of darkness and expanding of light as we drew close to the summer solstice. The assignment worked because I had made the exact number of scaled pages to encompass the vacation. I didn't want to end up with blank pages, so I felt compelled to work away at my journal every single day. It also worked because once I had recorded sunrise and sunset I wanted to keep going, and I ended up drawing, painting, and writing many details that summarized each day.

Dana Fox Jenkins, *End of the Alphabet, the Annual Clique Weekend, and A Meeting in Boston*, 2004. 11 x 14 inches (27.9 x 35.6 cm). Acid-free and 100% cotton paper, watercolor, quick ink, stamps. Photo by Val Dunne

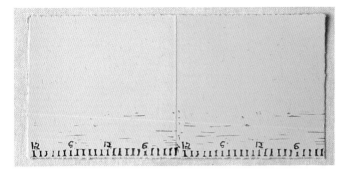

I began by stamping the scale of hours at the bottom of each page of the little journal.

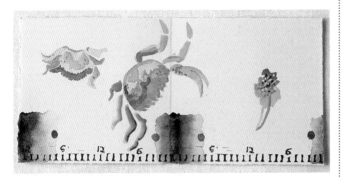

While outside, I painted small watercolors.

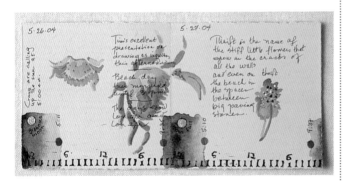

Later I wrote notes around and on top of the watercolors.

ALTERED BOOKS AND PAGES

An excellent starter is to use an old book for your journal. Alternately, you can add printed pages from an old book to a blank book or to a journal that you've made. The printed page, with its illustrations and type, sets the tone for the journal page. It might be a completely random selection or one from a book that means something to you. In either case, it will provide many points of entry and will give you a variety of images and words to build on or react against. When you're choosing a book to

Traci Bunkers, *I Have to Make Time to Take Care of Myself*, 2004. 11 x 17 inches (27.9 x 43.2 cm). Printed book altered with, gesso, marker, crayon, ink, photographs, thread, acrylic paint, transparency, copper tape; painted, glued, stitched, stamped with hand-carved rubber stamps. Photo by Image Works, Inc.

alter, consider the characteristics of the paper just as you would in buying a blank book (see page 14). If you're using a page that's extremely thin or fragile, it would be good to laminate it to a heavier page (see page 117).

Sometimes a base page from another book may need a little modifying. For example, if you've chosen to use a map with lines of about the same weight as the pen you'll be using, your writing is going to be hard to read. This might be the effect you're after, but if it's not, you can paint over the page (or parts of the page) with white or light-colored gouache. At first the gouache will seem to block out the underlayer completely. But as it dries, the print of the map will reappear in a lighter form than the original. When you write on it, your writing will come forward like a separate layer because it will be darker and sharper than the gouached-over map.

Gouache is good for pushing back or softening any layer or element that creates too much visual noise. The gouached-over element can still be deciphered to some extent, but it becomes a softer background message that no longer competes with what is put on top of it. Gouache is also useful for partially erasing or blotting out writing or drawing that you decide you want to erase or downplay. By applying several coats you can more completely obliterate the underneath layer. However, a ghost will always remain to create a nice palimpsest that hints at other, deeper layers of information just beyond reach (see Gouache on page 24).

Patterns Found and Lost

Sarah Midda is a British graphic designer who, in the early 1990s, spent a year in the south of France and kept a lovely illustrated diary about her experience. Midda's watercolors and pen and pencil sketches report on every aspect of life in the French countryside. She seems drawn to collections and patterns, and takes a particular delight in revealing easily overlooked details. It feels perfectly right that Midda picked up the orderliness and patterned nature of this place in her drawings and writing. Her small, flawlessly designed pages are a reflection of a place of gardens and fields with well-disciplined rows of lavender and sunflowers.[1]

Midda arranges her sketches on the page like chocolates in a box. Some pages are grids with each tiny box filled with a painting of an object. She imposes these patterns by first looking for them in an individual object or a grouping of objects. Typically, she draws and paints them, and then encloses the images in boxes. When she paints varieties of lettuce, for example, she arranges the drawings in a column five leaves high, puts text above and below the leaves, surrounds all the leaves with a red-ruled box, and paints what looks like the back of a seed packet as a frame for the whole arrangement.

Midda even turns colors into patterns. On several pages she paints a column of color boxes in the margin, and writes below where the colors are from: a stationery store, various table linens, a field of flowers. Her book is a great example of finding beauty and order,

yet not pinning it down like a trapped butterfly. Rather, all of her pages sparkle with light, and exuberance seems to spill and burst from the boxes in which the drawings are placed.

An Englishwoman named Muriel Foster kept a very different kind of journal. Foster created a diary that, from the beginning, disregarded the printed lines and columns on its pages and managed to lose and subvert most, if not all, sense of the pre-imposed pattern. The diary was never intended for publication, but was Foster's private record of her lifelong pleasure—fly-fishing. The first entry in her diary is September 16, 1913, and the last dated entry is June 1, 1949, around the time she was forced to give up fishing due to arthritis.

The book itself is a standard early 20th-century English fishing diary. It has

DATE	WHERE CAUGHT	WATER	RODS	FLY	SALMON	GRILSE	TROUT	SEA TROUT	VARIOUS	WEIGHT LBS.	OZS.
1923											
June 15	Eastbourne, Sussex		1 line.						2 Dabs		
July 5	Loch Broom Glebe	Loch an Tiompain	1				1				12
" 6	" " "	Loch a Charn		Silver Phantom			1			1	4
" 9	" " "	" " "	2	sunk flies			6			4	
" "	" " "	Loch an Fhiona	1	" "			2				8
" 10	" " "	Loch an Tiompain	1	Olive Dun			1				
" 11	" " "	" " "	1	" "							
" 12	" " "	" " "	1	" "			1				
" 16	" " "	Loch a charn	2	10 on double fly			12			5	4

From *Muriel Foster's Fishing Diary* by Muriel Foster, © 1980 by Patricia King. Use by permission of Viking Penguin, a division of Penguin Group (USA) Inc.

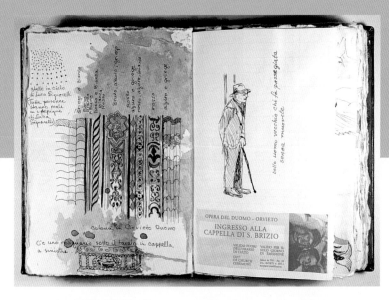

Gwen Diehn, *Untitled Journal Page*. 6 x 9 inches (15.2 x 22.9 cm). Pen, watercolor wash, and collage on handmade paper. Photo by Aleia Woolsey

ruled lines demarking columns for the date, where the fish was caught, the kind of water, the rods and flies used, the number of trout, salmon, grilse, sea trout, and various other fish caught, and the weight in pounds and ounces of each fish. The facing page is titled "remarks" and has a red line ruled the width of the page under the title.

Foster neatly records the date and usually fills in the "where caught" column, as well as frequently filling in other columns. But beginning with the first page, she adds sketches of subjects, such as swimming ducks, fish, or the flies she uses. Sometimes her drawings overlap several columns, as on one page near the front of the diary where a sea otter swims in a pond that encompasses four columns, and another peeks over the red line on the facing page. Foster routinely uses the "remarks" page to do more developed paintings and drawings as well as integrate textual comments. She disregards lines sometimes and at other times makes the red line become part of the design.

On one page, meticulously painted flies seem to be threaded on the red line separating salmon and grilse. On the facing page the horizontal red line bisects a pen drawing of Leckmelm Lodge, which she was visiting. Occasionally she paints a two-page spread, completely subverting the preprinted lines and text. On other pages she draws her own charts and superimposes them on the red lines, then finishes off the page with, for example, a few seagulls sitting on a barrel that bobs about in the bottom of the "where caught" and "water" columns.

If we can learn from Sara Midda the ways of seeing pattern and variety within everyday objects and how to assemble things into collections, we can learn from Muriel Foster how to make a pre-formatted book our own, how to bend it to our purposes. Foster also teaches us how to notice the many prosaic and mundane things that make up the tapestry of a long practice, how to express the flavor of a favorite pastime. Her text notes are occasionally more revealing of her emotions than are her drawings, which tend to remove them from the objects drawn.

One day in May, 1929, she writes, "Lost the fish of my life! Saw him jump out of the water thought it was a grilse—trolled over him & hooked him. He ran out a tremendous line, came up and lashed on the surface & broke me & took my minnow! Jimmy thought him an 8-pounder!"[2] The next two pages are completely without notes. A watercolor painting of a lake and hills fills both pages. The red lines hover over the hilltops. Maybe she took a day off from fishing after the 8-pounder got away!

[1]Sarah Midda. *South of France*. NY: Workman Publishing, 1990.

[2] Patricia King. *Muriel Foster's Fishing Diary*. NY: The Viking Press, 1980.

Inside the illustration:
LA LLUVIA
ARENAL VOLCANO
LAKE ARENAL
HOT SPRINGS

By far the wettest day of the trip. I woke... the roof of the hotel room. We spent the morning at Tabacon Hot Springs and ate lunch. We asked some folks from New Hampshire for a ride back to our hotel, where we got ready for an afternoon walk to the lava fields until it began to pour buckets and we became a view of Lake Arenal. It began soaking wet "empapada", socks, shoes, coats, pants, everything drenched

Jane Dalton, *Manipura*, 2003. $8^{1}/_{2}$ x 6 inches (21.6 x 15.2 cm). Acid-free paper, colored pencils, gel pen. Photo by Aleia Woolsey

Middles

There are a number of good ways to proceed after you've begun a page. Often you'll begin the page when you're on site and then do a middle layer later on, either at home that night or even on the plane flying back from a vacation. Sometimes middles become reflections on or responses to the starter that you've done.

WRITING

In a visual journal, writing is often done on a page that is already headed in a particular direction, making the writing a part of the image-making process. In this sense, writing becomes a visual element as well as an encoded message.

By writing, we can name and extend our drawings, tell their significance, raise questions about them, add information, and also slow down the looking process, which makes the reader dwell longer on the page. Even if the writing is in a foreign language or is in some other way indecipherable, the presence of writing always suggests that a message exists, that some meaning could be constructed beyond the more obvious message or meaning of the visual.

Consider what happens when we write: we draw certain conventional shapes that, in combination, become signs that signal the reader to create meaning. Notice that it's the reader who creates the meaning. What the writer does is provide clues and signs that point the reader in a particular direction and toward a certain meaning. The reader brings his or her entire background to the event of making meaning out of the symbols on the page, just as the writer has brought a lifetime of experience to the writing.

SUBTRACTING TEXT

Writing can also be done as a process of elimination. If you begin with a piece of printed text, either from a book that you're altering or from a piece of ephemera that contains text, you can use a pen or brush to gradually eliminate words until all that is left is the message you want to convey. These remaining words will form a piece of found poetry, and you'll be surprised at the results.

The process of eliminating words allows you to sneak up on expression. Instead of laboring to find the perfect way to say something, you simply float along on a sea of words, grabbing those that appeal to you or that seem to advance the meaning you've set out to communicate. You can rewrite the poem as you play around with spacing, letter shapes, and color, working on the poem or short passage until it feels right.

Charlotte Hedlund, *Untitled Journal Page,* **2003. 8 x 6 inches (20.3 x 15.2 cm). Bound journal, book page on bristol board, PVA glue, micro beads, acrylic paint, ink; collaged, glued, and painted. Photo by artist**

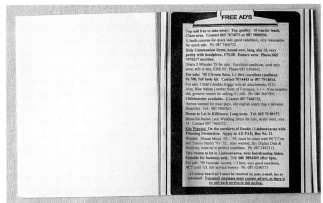

I began by laminating a found sheet of text to the journal page.

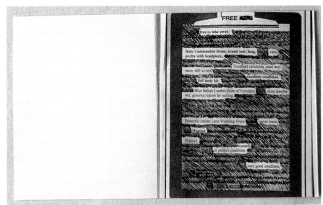

I then selectively marked out words with a black pen.

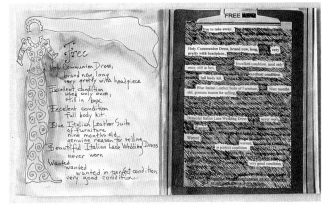

Finally, I copied the resulting poem onto the facing page, added a drawing, and washed on some light watercolors.

In the example shown above to the right, I started with a page from an advertisement flyer. I was attracted to it because it was so much a part of the community I was visiting. The oddness of some of the objects for sale especially intrigued me. Using a glue stick, I laminated the flyer to my journal page. Later, after I had selected certain words and phrases, I felt that my abridgment of the page took on a more universal meaning and became a comment about wanting and seeking. I would never have thought of writing this poem had I started with a blank piece of paper.

Rebecca Johnson, *The Sad People Parade*, 2004. 11 1/2 x 12 inches
(29.2 x 30.5 cm). Handmade journal, watercolor, photographs, beeswax

EXTENDING COLLAGE

A low-risk way to start drawing, as well as a way to bring your journal page along, is to start with a small collage and then extend it with your own drawing or painting. Here's how it works: Gather your ephemera. When you're ready to work in your journal, attach one of these gleanings to a page. Now take a pen or colored pencil, or whatever seems good to you at the moment, and extend the object or what's printed on the object. For example, you might start out by tearing a photograph in half and drawing in the other half. You may get wild and invent the second half to better express what you're really thinking or feeling. In the example shown at the top of page 85, I glued pressed flowers to a page with a glue stick and then extended them so that they became actually rather monstrous, a good expression of my overgrown garden after a month away from home during a rainy season. After the drawing was finished, I painted over the pressed flowers with matte-finish polymer varnish to seal them to the page. I did this after and not before drawing because polymer varnish isn't a good surface for watercolors.

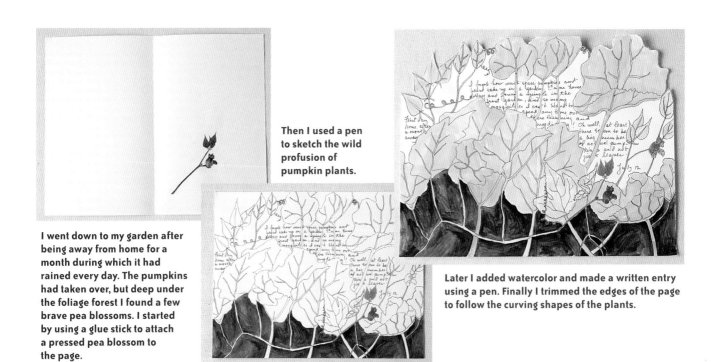

Then I used a pen to sketch the wild profusion of pumpkin plants.

I went down to my garden after being away from home for a month during which it had rained every day. The pumpkins had taken over, but deep under the foliage forest I found a few brave pea blossoms. I started by using a glue stick to attach a pressed pea blossom to the page.

Later I added watercolor and made a written entry using a pen. Finally I trimmed the edges of the page to follow the curving shapes of the plants.

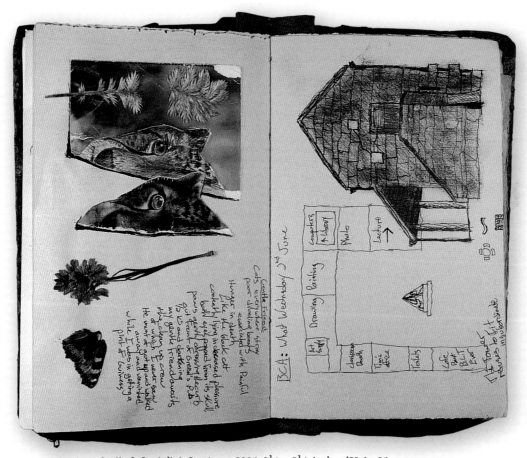

Justin S. Cantalini, *Creatures*, 2004. 8¹/₂ x 5¹/₂ inches (21.6 x 14 cm). Hand-bound journal, handmade paper, found postcard, ebony pencil, butterfly wings, pressed orchid (Ireland), white craft glue, ink; written, drawn, glued, cut and pasted postcard, and collaged. Photo by Aleia Woolsey

Ivy Smith, *My Irish Bedroom*, 2004. 11¹/₄ x 9 inches (28.6 x 22.9 cm).
Bound journal, liquid acrylics, ink, watercolor. Photo by Aleia Woolsey

DRAWING

Drawing is another obvious way to work at the middle stage. If you don't consider yourself an artist, you may balk at this suggestion. But before deciding to skip this section, consider how we teach drawing in our culture. We don't teach many people how to draw because, too often, we equate drawing with artistic talent rather than seeing it as a basic human skill that is truly within everyone's reach.

If you've ever watched a young child draw, you know that drawing is as much a drive in children as speaking, reading, and writing. However, the reason most children go on to learn how to speak, read, and write fluently is that we teach these skills and expect everyone to learn them. But we don't expect everyone to learn how to draw. As soon as children begin to struggle to draw what they see, we decide they aren't "talented," and we point them in other directions instead of giving them the few instructions needed to get them over the hurdle. The rare children who happen to be precocious in drawing we

brand "artistic" and provide them and only them with instruction. (If we taught only precocious writers how to write, calling them poets or writers from the start, and told everyone else to forget about writing, most adults would be as unable to write as they are to draw.)

The more you draw, the better your drawings will be. To draw accurately you must learn how to see accurately. If you consider drawing to be an exploration, a kind of visual note taking, and if you're more interested in the process than in producing works of art, you will become a very accurate drawer. If you want to speed up the process of learning, check out *Drawing on the Right Side of the Brain* by Betty Edwards. This book, first published many years ago, has become a classic in the field of drawing instruction. I can think of no better tool to help you draw on your own.

Drawing will connect you to what you draw in a way that snapping a photograph never can. For one thing, drawing requires time and focus. It requires that you slow

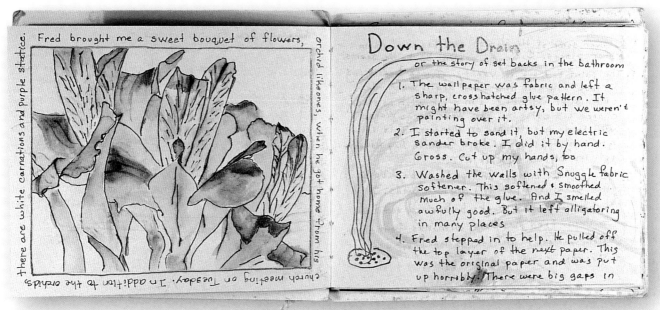

Edie Greene, *Untitled Journal Page,* **2003. 4 ³/₄ x 11 inches (12 x 27.9 cm).Hand-bound journal, computer paper, pen and ink drawing on sketch paper, watercolor wash, gel pen; glued and illustrated. Photo by Aleia Woolsey**

down and spend time with the object—that you analyze the way the parts fit together. In the process, you become aware of the grace and beauty of the most common object and place. You enter into a kind of unmediated communication with the subject of your drawing, and when you look back at your drawings months or years later, the events at the time of the drawing will rush back—you'll remember the weather, the conversation at the next table, how tight your new shoes were, and how good the breeze smelled. When you draw, nothing comes between you and what you are seeing—no camera lens, no interpretive guide book, no docent or tour guide telling you what to look at, no video selecting the aspects of a place for you to focus on. (See Drawing Accurately on page 54.)

Draw in your journal. Draw small things at first—parts of bigger things, patterns on things, outlines of interesting shapes. Start with the general, large form and work to the particular, the details. Take a few measurements—length versus width for example—and sketch in the general proportions. Then fill in smaller and smaller parts. Draw whatever interests you. Draw what confuses you or who confuses you. Draw the same thing every day for a week and see what happens. Draw the same changing thing, such as a plant, every day for a month and see what happens, both to the plant and to your drawing skills. Draw with a pencil, a pen, a marker, or a crayon.

See the effect of different drawing tools on your drawings. Check out artist Danny Gregory's website (www.everydaymatters.net) and study his book, *Everyday Matters* (NY: Princeton Architectural Press, 2003), to find inspiration from someone who has inspired hundreds of people to take up drawing.

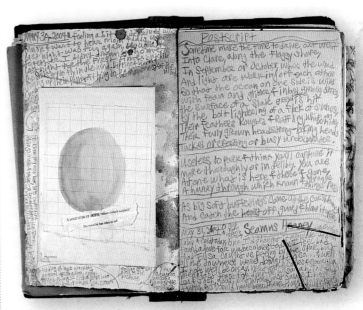

Clare Duplace, *Untitled Journal Page,* **2004. Splattered painted paper with writing and painted sun. Photo by Aleia Woolsey**

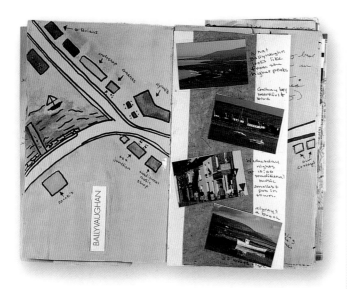

Megan Gulledge, *Untitled Journal Page*, 2004. Watercolor, pen, collage. Photo by Aleia Woolsey

MAPPING

We've talked about using maps as a background to set a particular context for whatever else happens on the page. Mapping is also a good process to use to record information during the middle stages. Drawing your own map lets you experience a place in a profoundly different way than looking at someone else's. Once you've mapped a place, whether it's as small as the top of your desk or as large as your neighborhood, you know many things about it that you didn't know before.

Since it's impossible to put everything in a map, the act of mapping is an act of selection, and that implies choices based on your point of view or area of interest. You will have to be selective. What do you want your map to show? Maps can be drawn for the purpose of recording a place. They can also be made to show directions. They can be projections or plans, a way of recording ideas for a new building or a rearranged room, a garden, or a city center.

The maps in your journal don't have to be accurate or to scale unless you want them to be. They might be maps that you make while you're walking somewhere, such as little records of which flowers are blooming this week in the woods near your house. They might be

drawn to scale if they are going to be used as plan drawings to help you decide how much paint or tile to buy for the addition to your house that you're planning.

In the example shown below, two students on a college field course had encountered a small deserted village in rural Ireland. They were interested in discovering the layout of the village—not an easy task, as it was overgrown with trees, bushes, ferns, mosses, and vines. In order to map it, they walked around the perimeter of the village several times, pacing off the various areas. Once they had a rough outline, they were able to begin to make sense of the low stone walls, which were all that were left of the houses and stables. They discovered what seemed to be a central green or square, the remains of a surrounding wall, and a number of small structures. They also discovered the remains of trees and plantings that gave clues as to how the land was perhaps once used. When they compared the maps they had made separately, they were pleased to note many concurrences and points of agreement. They learned much more about the village than they would have had they simply snapped a few photographs and moved on to something else.

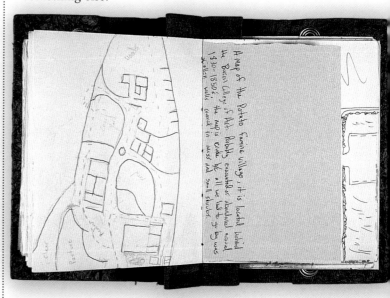

Matt Rogers, *Ireland Journal Page*, 2004. 5 x 5 ½ inches (12.7 x 14 cm). Hand-bound journal, ink. Photo by Aleia Woolsey

PAINTING

Sketchbook or journal painting can be thought of as drawing in color. If you're a little insecure about getting the proportions right, start out by using a pencil to measure (see page Drawing Accurately on page 54) and then lightly sketch the overall dimensions of the object or scene you want to paint. Next, put away the pencil. Then follow these two easily mastered practices to get you on the road to being comfortable with drawing in watercolor. First, know that if you paint over wet paint, your outlines will be fuzzy and diffused. If you want crisp definition, you must wait for the paint to dry completely before painting over it. Secondly, always start with the general shape and the lightest color and move to the particular details and the darkest shade.

Let's see what this looks like in action. Let's say I want to paint a small building that I can see across a field. Quickly I measure to find the relationship of its height to its width. I use a pencil to lightly sketch in a rectangle to reflect that relationship. I might also make a few other marks to indicate where the door is in relation to the chimney, how high the roof is relative to the height of the wall from ground to roof bottom, etc. Next, I mix up a light color that seems to underlie all the colors of the building, here a pale yellow. I brush a diluted coat of this watercolor all over the rectangles and roofs (see figure 1),

and let it dry until the paper is no longer cool or damp to the touch. This will take a few minutes. While I'm waiting for the paint to dry, I analyze the colors to determine the next darkest color that is on the building. I mix up that color and paint it all over the building except in those places where I need the pale yellow to show (see figure 2). While that coat is drying, I determine the next darkest color, and so on until I have painted the smallest, darkest details and the building is complete (see figure 3).

Layered painting such as this can be done with any subject matter. Over time you'll grow more and more skillful in mixing colors and in deciding exactly where to place colors and where to leave the underlying color showing through. Note that you won't use your darkest colors until the very end, and then only in the few places where the subject is truly that dark.

There are many books to help you learn watercolor painting on your own. Most important, however, is practice. As with drawing, painting puts you in direct contact with the subject. The process slows you down and makes you pause, reflect, focus, truly look, and reconsider the mental stories you tell about what you think you see. (See Watercolors on page 19 to 20 to learn more about paint mixing and handling.)

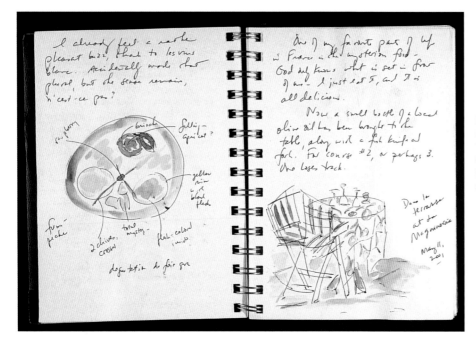

Faith McLellan,
In Provence, 2000.
7¹/₂ x 5¹/₂ inches
(19 x 14 cm). Bound journal,
ink, watercolor; painted
and written. Photo by artist

RELIEF PRINTS AND RUBBINGS

Relief prints and rubbings both make use of the same principle: a relief or design that's raised above a flat surface prints, whereas the recessed background doesn't. In making relief prints, you apply paint or ink to the relief areas of the printing block only, and then transfer that to a piece of paper by means of pressure. In a rubbing, the relief areas provide resistance when you rub the whole area with a crayon or pencil, yielding a print of the relief area.

The world is filled with relief textures, and it's easy to do rubbings, even in a bound journal. Keep your eyes open for textures, beginning with the ever-popular tombstones and moving onto water main and sewer covers, embossed plaques and labels, tree bark, textured wallpaper, pressed plant parts, seashells, pottery shards, coins, etc. To do a rubbing, press the page or piece of paper flat against the surface, attaching it with small pieces of masking or drafting tape to keep it from moving around. Then use the broad side of a piece of crayon, graphite stick, or even the side of a pencil point, and gently stroke over all the area. Gradually the relief areas begin to show up and the recessed areas remain either uncolored or become only lightly colored. If your journal paper is too thick to do a good rubbing, or if the binding makes it too awkward to carry out the process, do your rubbings on separate, thinner paper and laminate or tip them into the journal afterwards.

A relief print is made from a piece of wood, linoleum, or eraser-like material on which the design area stands up from the rest of the surface. A fingerprint is a simple example of a relief print because it's the ink attaching itself to the ridges of our fingers that makes the print possible. You can make your own small

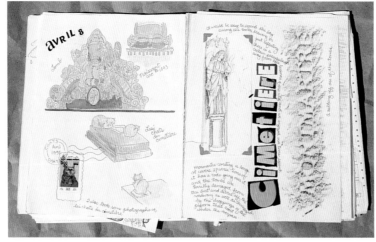

Judy Rinks, *Paris Travel Journal*, 1998. 8 ¹/₂ x 11 inches
(21.6 x 27.9 cm). Bound journal, graphite stick, watercolor, ink, paper
scraps, postage stamp, pencils; drawn, painted, rubbed,
and glued. Photo by artist

Gwen Diehn, *Untitiled*, 2004.
6 x 7 inches (15.2 x 17.8 cm). Journal made
with an old book cover, handmade paper, gouache,
eraser print, watercolor, pen.

relief printing blocks, or stamps, using rubber or plastic erasers, corks, or even foam earplugs. You might try carving an alphabet or numerals or make stamps of motifs or designs from the environment about which you are writing and drawing.

To make a stamp, use a black pen to draw the shape onto a cork or eraser or piece of rubber stamp-carving material. Remember that the print will be a reverse of the stamp, so be sure to draw letters and numerals in reverse. Then use linoleum carving tools or a razor knife to cut away the background, leaving the design area raised, or "in relief." Corks may need to be lightly sanded before carving or have a thin slice removed if they have bumpy ends. You can carve the rounded sides of a cork as well as its flat ends. If you don't generate sufficient used corks from your own bottles, you can buy corks from hardware stores.

Buy stamp pads from craft supply stores—keep in mind that while dye-based inks dry faster than pigment-based inks, they will bleed through some papers. The pigment inks tend to be more opaque and more intense in color. The people in the craft supply store will usually be happy to explain the differences among all the myriad kinds of stamp pads they sell.

Stamped prints can be used alone, in borders, and even to design entire backgrounds or page surfaces. Relief prints are a low-tech process and often seem to have a somewhat old-fashioned look. They're frequently used to evoke nostalgia, and, conversely, they are often used ironically. They are often very effective when juxtaposed with more high-tech materials, such as crisp black pen lettering. They are also very useful for carrying a recurring motif throughout a book.

A collection of homemade stamps carved from test-tube stoppers

Toppings

Going back to edit and rework your journal allows you the opportunity to mine a repository of ideas. Even a journal that was originally intended to be a private record of daily happenings and emotions can provide information and images that become the seeds of future artwork and writing. You'll also want to go back sometimes and finish some things that you were unable to complete on site. Look for unfinished drawings, outlines and lists that seem to need expansion, questions that you've posed, and drawings and paintings that could use written explanation.

Especially seek out pages that seem hopeless, pages that you wish you had never written, failed drawings, pathetic attempts at mapping, or boring collages. These bad pages make the best grist for your mill. It's easier to take risks and try out new processes and approaches with them because there's nothing to lose— even if you just make more of a mess. Toppings are ideas for going back—for enhancing, expanding, finishing, erasing, morphing, even completely obliterating the images and information you've gathered.

Gwen Diehn, *Untitled Journal Page*. Watercolor, gouache, fluid acrylic, and pen on handmade paper. Photo by Aleia Woolsey

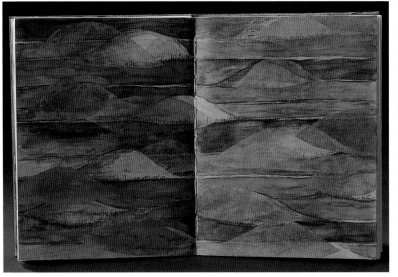

Nancy Pobanz, *Untitled Journal Page*, 2002. 9⁷/₈ x 15¹¹/₁₆ inches (25.1 x 39.8 cm). Coptic bound journal, handmade paper, fabric, black and maroon ink, soil pigment, acrylic matte medium, magazine clipping; hand written, drawn, painted, collaged, and glued. Photo by Lightworks Photography

WRITING

It's a good idea to bring your journal up to date as frequently as possible. Writing is often the first and easiest way to expand the information in a drawing or map. Even if you took notes on site while making the drawing, take time to review and add to them as soon as you get home so you don't forget important details and ideas. If you didn't leave a space for your writing when you made your painting or drawing, you can write right on top of it. Or, try making your writing part of the design by using the writing for a border around the page or by placing it in a box within the image. When using poured or pre-painted paper, the paper itself will often suggest places where you can tuck your writing.

This was a page that already had poured fluid acrylics on it.

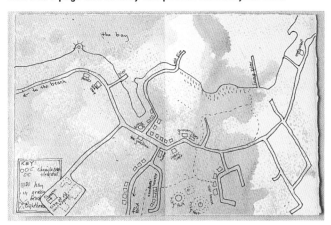

I drew a map and wrote some captions.

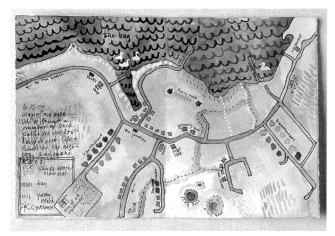

Next I added watercolor tones, textures, and details.

WATERCOLOR WASHES

Another easy and natural topping, one that will add color to your pages, is to add a watercolor wash to a drawing or a map. If you've used a waterproof pen, the wash will have no effect on the lines of your drawing. If you've used a pen that will run when it has a wash put over it, use colored pencils to add color. Or, let the running of the drawing ink be a part of the design. Use color behind writing and in the spaces behind and around small drawings. Alternatively, you might use a strip of colored boxes at the bottom or side of a pen drawing to show the colors associated with the drawing or place.

You can also use watercolor washes to organize a cluttered page. Use different colors to create columns, a grid, or abstract shapes that will put emphasis on parts of the page and lower the intensity of others.

ELIMINATING WORK

Sometimes you just want to get rid of what you've done. Gouache, depending on whether or not you dilute it, will completely or partially obliterate what you've done. Even if you paint just a light coat of gouache over some writing or drawing, the gouache will lighten your work and will reduce the contrast between the paper and the ink or paint so that you can overpaint or overwrite clearly (see Gouache on page 24).

Another way to get rid of something is to use a pen to draw fine lines of texture over the area you want to obscure. You can weave the words you don't want to see into a mesh of lines that can't be read. As a last resort you can always cut the page out and turn it into a stub to which you can attach another sheet of paper or an envelope.

SEPARATING LAYERS

Sometimes a page, especially in a layered journal, has good information but seems cluttered and full of visual noise. A remedy for this problem is to separate layers. One way to do this is to raise elements so that they seem to float above the surface of the page. You can do this easily by painting a shadow under the element. Another similar layer separator is to first box in drawings and then add shadows under the boxes. When you write, let

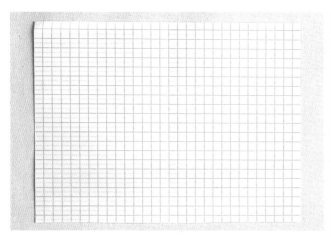

Visiting the grave of writer Flannery O'Conner, I wanted to do a journal entry about her and about that hot July day spent with my family in Milledgeville, Georgia. I started with a sheet of grid paper that was already bound into the journal.

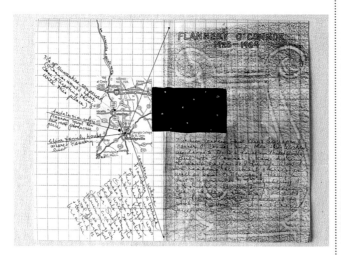

I did a gravestone rubbing using a dark blue crayon furnished by my niece, Grace.

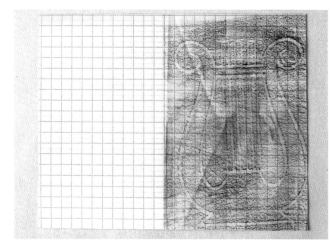

I finished the page by drawing and annotating the map, writing a journal entry around the rubbing, and painting a dark blue night sky "hole" in the page with Payne's gray acrylic.

it go right up to the edge of the box, stop, and continue on the other side. This gives the appearance of a line of text that travels beneath the box (see page 44).

Another way to separate out layers is to use metallics or warm tones to add light to a page. Metallic and warm-colored areas seem to come forward visually. If you think a collage or other visual will appear cluttered if you write over it with a black pen, consider using a gold or silver pen. Try painting a metallic or golden-yellow background behind a visual. Using a metallic pen to emphasize an initial letter or to box in a visual will draw the eye to that spot.

Besides raising layers you can also lower them. A wash of a cool color, such as a blue-gray, will make an area appear to sink a little below the level of the rest of the page. To punch a deep "hole" in a page, draw a box or other shape where you want the hole to be and fill it with a very dark color (you can overwrite with silver or white ink). Alternatively, draw a box around an element and paint a very dark background around the drawing in the box.

Of course, you can literally cut holes in the pages to link one to another. This process takes some advanced planning—you don't want to cut a hole that will remove something from the other side of the page. This technique is an interesting way to build continuity between pages. A related idea is to trim the edges of one page so that material on the next page is visible.

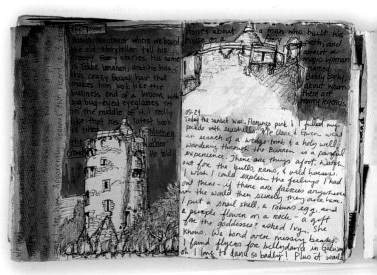

Miriam McNamara, *Journal Page*, 2004. Bound journal, ink pen, colored pencil, acrylic paint. Photo by Aleia Woolsey

Journaling with Children

Jacob Diehn, *Untitled Journal Page*, 2004. 6 x 10 inches (15.2 x 25.4 cm). Watercolor paper, watercolor, and pen. Photo by Sarah Bourne

hen my eldest son was in kindergarten, he came home from school one day with a well-worn little book that was made out of red construction paper, stapled along one edge, and embellished with a crayon drawing that included tentacles, many eyes, and six large circles. The book was not an object of great beauty, but it was clear from its condition that it was well used. He plopped it down on the kitchen table and asked me to tell him the date. I did, and he proceeded to slowly print "March 13" at the top of an empty page.

He explained to me that this was his journal, and that he had not finished working in it that day and needed to do it at home. He then began to draw, explaining what was going on in his picture as he worked. When he finished, he gave the book to me and asked me to write down the story he was going to tell me about his drawing. He began to dictate: "This is my truck that I lost but now I found it this morning." After I wrote the words, he took the book back and copied each word beneath the words I had written.

Because children love to draw and tell stories, making illustrated journals comes naturally to them. All it takes is an interested adult or older child. After the child draws an event of the day, have him or her tell you about it and write down the words. One or two sentences are enough. If the child is learning to write, leave space for him or her to copy the words underneath. This is a great way to help a child to read. Children are extremely motivated to read back the words they have "written," and

before long they'll be able to write on their own without needing to dictate or copy the words.

Travel journals are great fun for children and their families. These can be either individual journals or group journals with entries added by everyone in the traveling group. I remember a journal that one of my sons kept during a long car trip. The first few pages consisted of lines that looked like the tracings of a seismograph. When asked about these strange lines, he explained that he had rested his pencil lightly on the page and let the motion of the car draw the line while the car was moving, and every time we hit a bump the line got wiggly. His lines were a record of the movement of the car during certain segments of the trip. Another son kept a record of out-of-state license plates during a long drive across country.

My neighbor and his 12-year-old son took a road trip from the east coast out to California. Both father and son kept illustrated journals to record the trip—the waves they surfed, the beaches visited, memorable meals, unbelievable sights. Because the son was old enough to write reflectively as well as draw and paint, the journal contained

reflections about the experience as well as a narrative of events.

My five-year-old grandson and I have journals that we work in together on our regular Sunday morning outings. Our usual practice is to go to breakfast at our favorite grocery store/café, and paint and write in our journals while we sit at the table. Sometimes we draw and write our plans for the rest of the morning. Other times we record what we see going on around us in the café. Sometimes we wait and work in our journals while at the park or at the lake near his house. In the example shown, Jacob drew an ant house based on our observations of an anthill in a sidewalk crack in his front walkway. We had watched it for a while before setting off, and when we started working in our journals, he was still interested in that ant colony. He began by drawing, and then he asked me how to spell the words as he printed them on the page.

Another time, Jacob and I worked together on a page in my travel journal while we were on vacation together. I had drawn a map as the basis of the page, and he added his own map to the center of my map. We added watercolor to the page together. (see page 6)

Betsy Couzins, *True Work*, 2003, 8½ x 11 inches (21.6 x 27.9 cm). Watercolor paper, watercolors, photographs, ephemera, labels, markers. Photo by artist

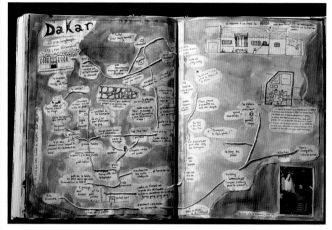

Aude Iung-Lancrey, *Memory Map*, 2004. 17 x 11 inches (43.2 x 27.9 cm). Bound journal, matte medium, acrylic paint, yarn, ink, photograph; glued and collaged. Photo by David Swift

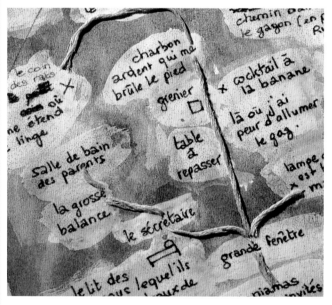

Detail, Aude Iung-Lancrey, *Memory Map*.

COLLAGE AS A LINK

A final idea for a topper is to use collage to link elements or to create a focal point. Collage can be used as a starter or middle for a page, and it can also be used as a final element, the one that calls attention to itself. If the collage is a pressed flower or leaf, a piece of newspaper, or any other fragile element, it's a good idea to coat it with a layer of polymer varnish in order to seal it from the air and to protect it from the friction of page turning. Any element sealed this way will last for years on a page. If you use matte-finish varnish, you will not be able to see the varnish once it is dry.

Collaborations and Group Journaling

Traci Bunkers, *The Scales Have Tipped to Happiness (from An Ongoing Conversation with Juliana Coles)*, 2004. 10 x 20 inches (25.4 x 50.8 cm) open. Children's book, pinhole Polaroid photos, acrylic paints, postage stamps, paper scraps, transparency, ink, masking tape, labels, brads; collaged, painted, stamped, glued. Photo by the Image Works, Inc.

Traci Bunkers and Julianna Coles kept this journal as a prolonged conversation, mailing it back and forth for many months.

Keeping a group journal during a family vacation can be a means of enlarging everybody's experience. When people look at and read each other's entries, they see things they may have missed on their own. Those who have never kept an illustrated journal quickly learn from those with more experience. A good idea is to keep the group journal in a place where everyone can have easy access to it—the living room of the rental cottage or on the dresser in the hotel room. If that's not practical, people can take turns carrying the journal. Each person can have the journal for a day and then pass it on to the next person. At the end of the vacation, you can make copies of the journal for everyone in the group, including some blank pages at the back for people to add individual reflections on the trip as well as photographs—a very nice memento of the trip.

Pauses

As we've seen in the section How Does Your Journal See the World?, some people like a more spare, quiet way of working. If you're the keeper of a wabi-sabi journal or a naturalist's journal, you'll probably be more interested in simplicity than in the complexity that results from working in many stages or layers. For you, uncluttered, minimalist pages are more appealing, and the kind of pages that I am calling "pauses" may form the majority of the pages in your journal.

Even if the majority of the pages in your journal are complex and many-layered, there's nothing wrong with occasional single-layer pages, pages that signify a pause or just a quiet period. All of our days are not equally frantic, so consider including simple, uncomplicated, unlayered pages when the day seems to warrant them.

Today's visual journal sometimes seems to be on the forefront of a new form: the journal as artwork. In an interview with Chris Gage (mediabistro.com, June 8, 2004), journal-keeper and illustrator Danny Gregory says, "I create my art in journals. I document what goes on around me constantly."

If you're thinking of your journal as artwork in the form of a book, an art piece that will someday be leafed through and looked at by other people, then you might want to think in terms of overall design of the journal as well as that of the individual pages. Even though the genre of the journal may be less formal and consciously

Kelcey Loomer, *First Page*, 2003. 9¼ x 6¼ inches (23.5 x 15.9 cm). Journal, cutout from a children's encyclopedia, milkweed seeds, pen. Photo by Aleia Woolsey

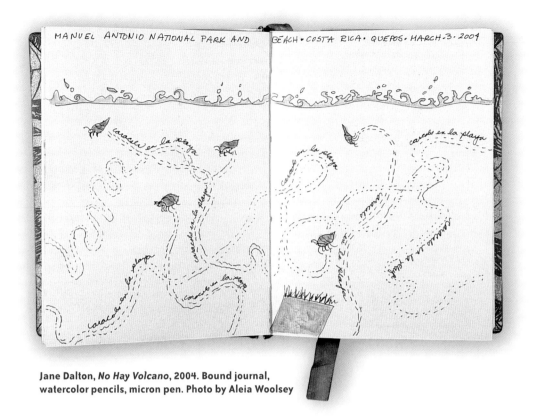

Jane Dalton, *No Hay Volcano*, 2004. Bound journal, watercolor pencils, micron pen. Photo by Aleia Woolsey

designed than that of other artists' books, it's still good to provide some rhythm to the overall work by putting in some occasional pauses in the form of minimally-worked pages. Such pauses are the equivalent of rests in music.

Simple pages can slow down the rhythm of the book, invite introspection, and provide a rest. Even if you don't think of your journal as book art and never plan to show it to anyone else, as the writer/artist you need some rest, too. Instead of skipping those days when you're too busy to spend much time on the journal, make a plain page. A particular day might need only a few lines scrawled across a light blue ground or a small drawing perfectly centered and unembellished. Also consider blanks, pure pattern pages, text-only pages, single small images, and other uncomplicated pause pages.

Remember, the object isn't to turn your journal into something as bulky as a roofing-tile sample book. Paper is a relatively light and fragile support. A book is generally a handheld object, and as such it's improved by being comfortable to hold and pleasant to manipulate. Journals are handled much more than most other books, so these principles especially hold true for them.

The Reluctant Bookbinder

If you're on a quest for the perfect journal—one with the right color and texture and weight of paper, the perfect size, the perfect eccentricities of style—this section might be just what you need. Even if you have no interest in learning how to bind books, and all the fussy details of bookbinding make you cringe, you'll be pleasantly surprised to learn that you can make your own journals with a minimum of equipment, time, and skill.

Basics

The most important element of a visual/verbal journal is the paper, and the choice is completely under your control when you make your own book. In fact, getting the paper you want is probably what has driven you to the extreme of learning to make your own journal, so we'll begin here. First, go to art supply, craft, stationery, office supply and wrapping paper stores, or even old map dealers to find your papers. Consider combining plain white unlined papers with old maps, sheets of brown craft paper, grid paper, or sheets of colored vellum—let your imagination be the guide. Imagine what it would be like to write on buttery yellow handmade Thai paper, crisp elegant resume paper, or even wrinkled pages torn from an old atlas.

After the text pages, the cover is the next most important element. The cover of a journal needs to be strong enough to protect and contain the text pages plus whatever ephemera—ticket stubs, small scraps of paper, photographs, postcards, etc.—that you gather and want to keep within the journal. So again, let your imagination roam freely. But realize that the cover will take something of a beating. You'll want to use paper or other material without fragile embellishments, such as embedded flower parts (unless you want to coat the cover with a varnish, which is also a possibility; see The Three-Minute Pamphlet Variations and Options on page 102). Since all the journals made in this section have soft covers, you want to find heavy, cover-weight paper, or leather that can be folded.

I added a pocket to the back of this beach journal. It gave me a place to store the small pamphlet journal that I used for sketching when I didn't want to carry the big journal.

The Three-Minute Pamphlet

The easiest to make, and most basic of books is a single-signature pamphlet. Once you've cut or torn the pages and cover, you can sew it in three minutes. Once you know how to make this little book, you can try some options to the basic style in order to customize the journal. For simplicity's sake, directions are given for a book that is 3 inches wide x 4 inches high (7.6 x 10.2 cm), but you can make the book any size you want.

TOOLS & MATERIALS

Text paper*

Cover paper, slightly heavier than the text pages, and slightly larger than each sheet of text paper

Ruler for measuring and tearing paper

Matt knife for cutting paper

Pushpin or awl

Pencil

An old telephone directory or other thick magazine, such as an old catalog

1 yard (.9 m) of heavy sewing thread, bookbinder's thread, embroidery floss, lightweight string, or even dental floss

Straight sewing needle with an eye large enough for the thread used

4 large paper clips

*You will need a sheet big enough to cut or tear into a sheet 6 (w) x 4 (h) inches (15.2 x 10.2 cm). Each sheet will be folded in half widthwise. To make a bigger book, start with a larger sheet of paper.

INSTRUCTIONS

1 Using the ruler or matt knife, tear or cut the text papers into 6 x 4-inch (15.2 x 10.2 cm) sheets, or whatever size you need. Make sure the width measurement is always double the finished page-width measurement you desire. The number of pages is determined by the thickness of the paper. For regular computer printer paper, for example, 8 sheets will work. For heavier paper, such as watercolor paper, 3 or 4 sheets will be all you can fold together before the papers begin to stick too far out at the edge and the fold becomes too rounded. Fold each sheet in half widthwise. Use a paper clip to smooth the crease of each sheet, as shown in figure 1 on page 101. Then nest the folded papers inside each other to form a pamphlet.

2 To make the cover, cut or tear a piece of slightly heavier paper to 6½ x 4⅛ inches (16.5 x10.5 cm). To accommodate different sizes of text paper, always cut the

cover ⅛ inch (3 mm) higher and ½ inch (1.3 cm) wider than the unfolded text pages. Fold the cover in half widthwise, and slip the text pages inside, as shown in figure 2.

3 Make the hole-punching pattern by first cutting a piece of scrap paper the height of the cover, here 4⅛ inches (10.5 cm), by 2 inches (5 cm) wide. Fold this strip in half lengthwise. Unfold it and then refold it in half top to bottom. Mark the center where the folds cross. Make two more marks, ½ inch (1.3 cm) down from the top and ½ inch (1.3 cm) up from the bottom, as shown in figure 3. Note: if your book is higher than 6 inches (15.2 cm), make two additional holes, each one midway between the center hole and top and bottom holes, as shown in figure 4.

4 To punch holes for sewing, open the telephone directory to a page near the middle—the telephone directory will hold the pamphlet in position while you punch the holes. Open the pamphlet, both cover and text pages, and center it on the open pages of the larger book. Place your hole-punching pattern in the crease of the pamphlet, pressing it in until it fits snugly in the crease, as shown in figure 5. Using the pattern as your guide, use a pushpin or awl to punch a hole in the fold of the pamphlet at each mark. Remove the pattern. Place a paper clip at the top and bottom of each side of the open pamphlet to prevent the pages from moving and to keep the holes lined up. Remove the pamphlet from the telephone directory.

5 Sew the pamphlet. Cut a piece of thread about 36 inches (91.5 cm) long, and thread the needle. Don't tie a knot yet. Poke the needle into the center hole from the outside of the pamphlet. Pull the thread through, being sure to pull parallel to the plane of the paper. You want to pull the thread gently, while making sure that it's tight.

Note: Do not pull straight up, or it will tear the paper. Leave a tail about 4 inches (10.2 cm) long (you can slip the tail under one of the paper clips to anchor it). Next, from the inside, poke the needle into either of the end

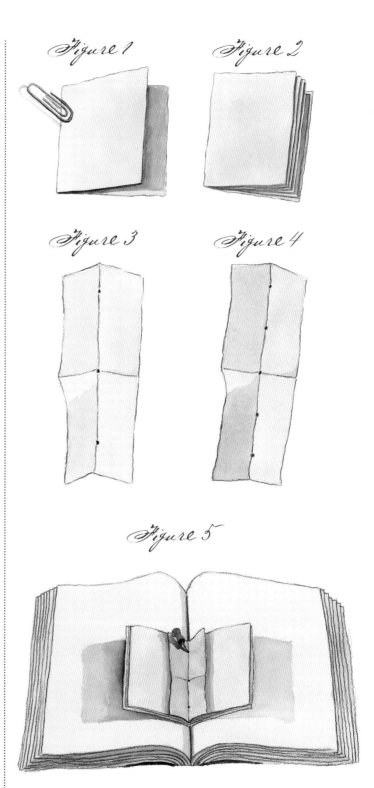

Figure 1

Figure 2

Figure 3

Figure 4

Figure 5

holes, and gently pull the thread tight. (Heed the warning above about pulling straight up!) Next, on the outside of the book, skip over the center hole, which has the tail coming out of it, and poke the needle into the remaining hole. Gently pull the thread tight. Finally, on the inside of the book, poke the needle back into the center hole, making sure that the needle comes out on the opposite side of the long stitch from the tail.

6 Tie the tail and the thread together in a double knot close to the hole, as shown in figure 6. Cut the threads to leave ends that are at least 1 inch (2.5 cm) long. You can also leave the ends longer for threading beads, or unravel the thread ends and braid them.

Note: If your book is higher than 6 inches (15.2 cm), follow figure 7 for your sewing pattern.

Variations and Options

Once you have the basics down and can make this journal in three minutes, you can easily make a few changes to the basic model:

- Consider cutting the cover paper a few inches wider than usual so that you can make cover fold-ins. By folding in this extra width, you will make the cover sturdier.

- Stitch the top and bottom edges of the cover fold-ins to make cover pockets.

- Slip a piece of cardboard between the front cover and the first page. Use a matt knife to cut a window in the cover. Put an illustration or title on the first page that can be seen through the cover window.

- Vary the width of the pages in the pamphlet. Long pages can be folded accordion-style to make fold-out pages. Short, 1-inch-wide (2.5 cm) pages can be used as stubs for gluing single sheets of paper, such as watercolor paper, color copies, or scans of photographs, fold-out maps, etc., as shown in figure 8.

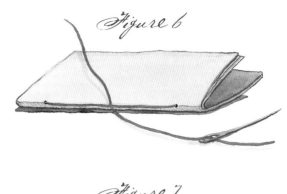

Figure 6

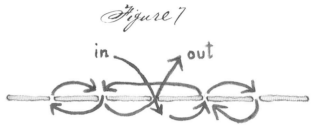

Figure 7

in   out

Figure 8

The Six-Minute Double Pamphlet

The only drawback to the three-minute pamphlet is that it's so small. However, once you've mastered that first reluctant foray into journal making, it's easy to simply double the number of pamphlets you fold to make a double pamphlet. There are two approaches to a double pamphlet given below. The first is called a *Dos à Dos*, meaning back to back; the second is a Pleat Book.

TOOLS & MATERIALS

2 booklets or pamphlets of folded text pages

Cover paper, ⅛ inch (3 mm) higher than the text pages and at least three times as wide

Needle and thread

Pushpin or awl

4 paper clips

Telephone directory or thick magazine

Pencil

Ruler

Matt knife

INSTRUCTIONS

1 For a *Dos à Dos*, fold the cover into a Z-shaped fold, as shown in figure 1 on page 104. For a Pleat Book, fold the cover so that it has a 1-inch (2.5 cm) pleat in the center, as shown in figure 2. Use the rounded end of the paper clip to *score* each fold. Scoring four or five times on the line of each fold makes it easier to get a precise fold. Burnish, or smooth, each fold using the rounded edge of the paper clip.

2 Make a hole-punching pattern, as described in step 3 for The Three-Minute pamphlet.

3 For either book, place an opened pamphlet into the first fold of the cover. As described in step 4 for The Three-Minute Pamphlet, place the cover and opened pamphlet in the center of the telephone directory or magazine. Press the pattern into the fold of the pamphlet, and punch the holes.

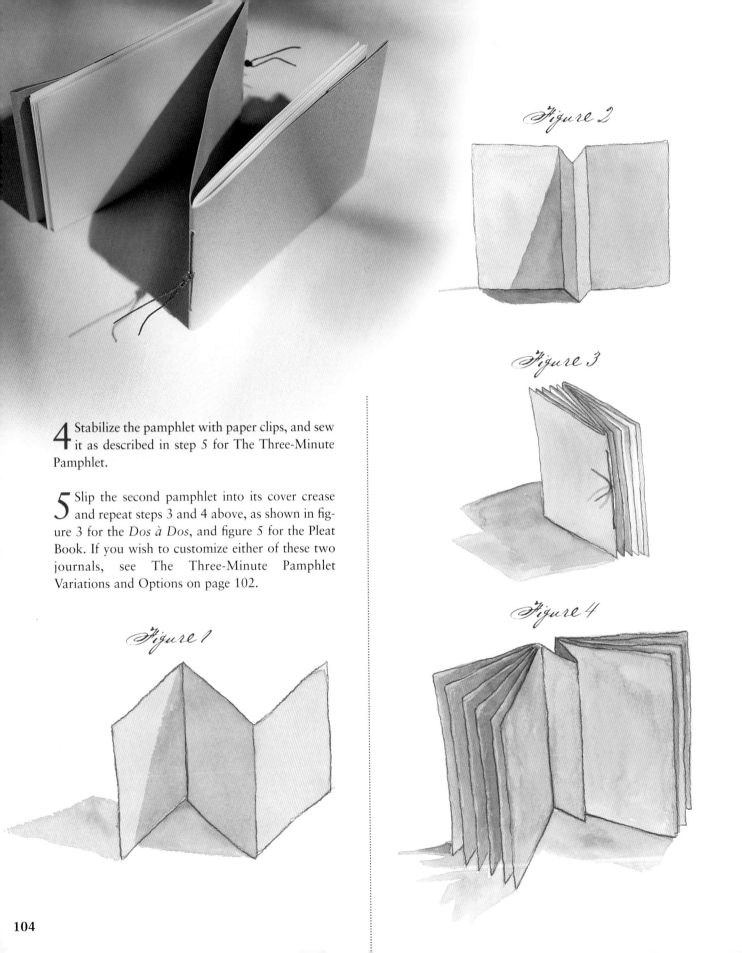

Figure 2

Figure 3

4 Stabilize the pamphlet with paper clips, and sew it as described in step 5 for The Three-Minute Pamphlet.

5 Slip the second pamphlet into its cover crease and repeat steps 3 and 4 above, as shown in figure 3 for the *Dos à Dos*, and figure 5 for the Pleat Book. If you wish to customize either of these two journals, see The Three-Minute Pamphlet Variations and Options on page 102.

Figure 4

Figure 1

Famous Reluctant Bookbinders

Paul Gauguin (1848-1903) *Album Noa Noa*. **Handwritten text and Polynesian woman seated. Photos by Herve Lewandowski, Reunion des Musees Nationaux/Art Resource, NY**

Reluctant bookbinding turns up in the most unlikely places. For instance, who would have expected Vincent Van Gogh to be a bookbinder? Yet not only did Van Gogh make some of his own sketchbooks, he also made several small accordion books that he filled with his drawings for the child of one of his friends. He wrote about the process to his brother Theo:

"However, for studies and scribbles the Ingres paper is excellent. And it is much cheaper to make my own sketchbooks in different sizes than to buy them ready-made. I have some of that Ingres paper left, but when you return that study to me, please enclose some of the same kind; you would greatly oblige me by doing so. But no dead white, rather the color of unbleached linen, no cold tones."[1]

Van Gogh's bookbinding method was simplicity itself—it got the job done, but didn't take a second longer than was necessary to produce the needed object. He would take a large sheet of suitable paper and fold it twice accordion style, with the folds going the length of the paper. Then he would fold the resulting long skinny rectangle in half with the fold going crosswise. It was an easy matter to put a few stitches in the final fold and trim the folds from the tops and bottoms of the pages. Voilà! A 12-page sketchbook made of his favorite warm white Ingres paper, ready to receive his notes and drawings.

Another reluctant bookbinder was Van Gogh's friend and fellow post-Impressionist painter, Paul Gauguin. When Gauguin moved to Tahiti and the Marquesas Islands, he was aware that he was the first European artist to live in a faraway land in order to discover the culture of a people who were then considered primitive and savage by Europeans. In 1894, while spending a few months in Paris before returning to the islands, he began a journal in order to explain what his stay in Tahiti had brought to his thinking and to his art. His journal began as a text manuscript, but he left spaces in the manuscript for illustrations, which he added later. He also went back into the manuscript after adding illustrations. From 1896 on, he kept notes and jottings about his daily life. During this period he also added woodcut prints and more illustrations. He bound the book himself, but it is no down and dirty, purely functional product. In the words of Victor Segalen, who collected Gauguin's mementos and was the first person to acquire the book from Gauguin's estate after his death:

"It is a volume of [white] pages, everything written on Ingres paper folded in quartos and sewn by the author, whose hand took delight in everything that becomes decorative material—wood skins, mother-of-pearl, wax and gold. The binding is supple and opens well under a tobacco-brown cover, velvety, without joins and flat-backed...The text, whose pale brown ink is in complete harmony with the browned paper, is, here and there, interrupted by watercolours-most of them washed on paper that has been separated, cut out and pasted. There are traces of everything which, at that time, made up the everyday life of the Master as he did battle with the merciless existence of the Tropics—the splendour of the light, hard work and renunciation."[2]

[1] *The Complete Letters of Vincent Van Gogh*, vol. 1, letter 164. Greenwich, Connecticut: New York Graphic Society, 1959.)

[2] Marc LeBot, *Gauguin's Noa Noa*, Assouline, 2004.

The Thirty-Minute Multiple-Pamphlet Journal

Building on the base of experience and confidence that you've gained by making single- and double-pamphlet books, you might want to venture a few steps further in complexity to make a journal that is many steps further in usefulness and beauty. A multiple-pamphlet journal uses the same skills you've gained in folding and sewing pamphlets, cutting, scoring, and folding covers, and in customizing journals; but it opens up the possibility of making the book as big and fat as you really want. It also introduces the possibility of making a hard cover for your journal.

TOOLS & MATERIALS

As many pamphlets as you want, with text pages cut and folded but not sewn.*
A piece of cover paper about five times the width of the text pages
Needle and thread
Pushpin or awl
Telephone directory or thick magazine
Ruler
Matt knife
Pencil

* Ten pamphlets are a likely limit when using most papers. More pamphlets than this will place undue stress on the spine of the book. (If you really want a bigger book, consider reinforcing the spine with a strip of cloth and a few more strips of paper.)

INSTRUCTIONS

1 Cut or tear, fold, and assemble as many pamphlets as you want.

2 Determine the thickness of the spine by piling up the pamphlets and *lightly* compressing them. Hold a ruler next to the stack. Write down the height of the stack of lightly compressed pamphlets. This will be the width of the spine of the book.

3 Follow figure 1 to determine the width of the cover paper. Make sure that the paper is ⅛ inch (3 mm) higher than the text pages. Cut or tear the paper to size. Score and fold all cover creases, as shown in figure 2.

4 Make a hole-punching pattern. Open the telephone directory or magazine. **Note:** For this book, place the pamphlet and cover flat on a page rather than into the center crease. Place the first pamphlet, or signature, opened out flat with its crease centered into the exact center of the spine section of the cover, as shown in figure 3. Lay the hole-punching pattern over the crease of the signature and punch the holes. Secure the signature to the cover with paper clips, and sew the first signature to the spine using the usual pamphlet stitch, as shown in figure 4.

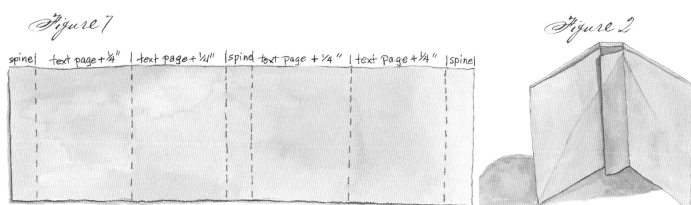

Figure 1

spine | text page + ¼" | text page + ¼" | spine | text page + ¼" | text page + ¼" | spine

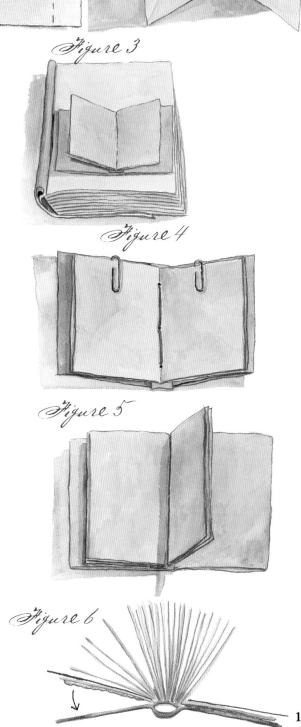

Figure 2

Figure 3

Figure 4

Figure 5

Figure 6

5 Close the first, sewn signature. Slide the second, closed signature either to the left or to the right of the first signature. From now on you will be sewing an equal number of signatures to the right and to the left of the center signature. Be sure to place them close enough so that they will all fit within the spine piece, as shown in figure 15. You might try placing the signatures before sewing to give you an idea of how close you can place them. Open the pamphlet, secure the pages with paper clips, punch holes, and sew each signature in turn. Trim the threads on the outside of the spine to ½ inch (1.3 cm).

Variations and Options

- To make a "hardback" book, use PVA to glue a piece of lightweight cardboard to the inside of each of the cover papers before folding the cover of the Thirty-Minute journal.

- To reinforce the spine of a very large book: Slip a piece of thin leather or heavy paper into the spine section between two of the layers of the cover paper that form the spine before sewing the signatures into the spine. Lightly glue the strip with PVA to one section of spine paper.

- For a sturdier spine and more formal, finished look, make a "new" cover out of an old hardback book cover. First remove the text pages (text block) from the old book. Using PVA and a glue brush, glue the outside covers of your Thirty-Minute Pamphlet (but *not* the spine) to the insides of the old cover, as shown in Figure 6. (For more directions see pages 122 to 123.)

You can also apply any of the options given for The Three-Minute Pamphlet Variations and Options on page 102.

The Art of Travel

By following the instructions in Francis Galton's book, I made a model of a sloppy-but-serviceable journal binding.

Poking around in a used bookstore one day, I came across a copy of a strange little guidebook for travelers. It had information ranging from how to thatch the roof of a temporary shelter, to what to pack when going trekking in the desert for six months, to how to repair a battered metal canteen using dried seeds. I stood there for nearly an hour learning how many pounds of gear a camel could carry versus a donkey, and what to do if my donkey brayed and I wanted to make him stop. (For those of you who must know: tie a stone to his tail because donkeys always lift their tails before braying, and if the tail is too heavy to lift, the donkey simply loses heart and won't bray.)

I had to have this book! I loved the odd title—*The Art of Travel* (1872): Or, *Shifts and Contrivances Available in Wild Countries*.[1] The author, Francis Galton, was writing for explorers and expeditionists primarily—although I learned that ordinary travelers had also bought his book in great numbers. There was information on every subject that I could imagine and many more. But what clinched the sale for me was the fact that the author devoted an entire chapter to the importance of and process of keeping a good journal during an expedition.

Galton suggested that the best journal notes were copious as well as accurate, and that these notes should be kept in a small but distinct handwriting. Hard pencils (HHH) on common paper were recommended. Not only should notes and observations and sketches be made on the spot, "in the exact order in which they occur," but these notes were then to be extended, expanded upon, and filled in each evening without fail—lest you forget important details and ideas. He tells about a famous explorer, Captain Burton, (short on candles, I assume) who managed to write in complete darkness. Burton would crawl into his sleeping bag, and then place a grooved piece of wood under his journal page so he could feel the grooves with his pen in order to stay on the lines.

Galton suggests the traveler keep three sets of books:

- Pocket memorandum measuring 3½ x 5 inches (8.9 x 12.7 cm) and made of strong paper with 150 pages in each. These are to be used for on-the-spot recording, and he expects the reader will need one of these every month.

- A logbook, which should be 5½ x 9 inches (14 x 22.9 cm) and filled with the printed forms of which Galton provides samples. He says the log book is useful for organizing information that might be scattered about in the pocket memo book, and the use of the printed forms simplifies things. There are two printed forms to be filled out each day and then two blank sheets for the compiling of the information that doesn't fit on the forms. One form is a grid, intended to be used for mapping and making diagrams. The other has spaces for information regarding the weather, compass readings, altitude, the nature of the country, and latitude and longitude.

• A calculation book, the same size as the logbook, is used for recording measurements from which calculations must be made—latitude and longitude, star positions relative to the moon, the length of the journey measured in time and converted to miles, etc.

Galton also gives instructions on what to do at the end of the journey. He tells the traveler to make drawings of everything that may not have yet been sketched— the equipment, the retinue, the encampment, and "whatever else you may in indolence have omitted to sketch." All loose items must then be pasted into the journals. Books must be stitched where they are torn. The notebooks should then be given to a bookbinder as soon as possible to rebind them and paginate them. The bookbinder should add plenty of extra pages to each book so that the traveler can write an index to the whole of the manuscript, including plenty of cross-references. The traveler should

add explanations where necessary and correct imperfect descriptions. It is imperative to do this immediately after the journey, Galton insists, because memories quickly fade once the traveler has returned home.

Because no stone is left unturned in this book, Galton also includes detailed directions for making ink out of charred sticks and milk, and carbon paper out of a mixture of soap, charcoal, and clean paper. He also included directions for binding books. He no doubt believed that some travelers would not have the means to have their journals professionally bound and did not want them returning home with unprotected notes.

A relative of Galton's developed a bookbinding form that Galton claims is not tidy looking but opens flat and never falls to pieces. After reading the instructions, I was compelled to make this book to see what a traveler's journal of this era, as interpreted by Galton, might actually look like. The results are pictured above. Following are Galton's instructions if you wish to attempt your own: "Take a cup of paste; a piece of calico or other cloth, large enough to cover the back and sides of the book; a strip of strong linen—if you can get it, if not, of calico—to cover the back; and abun-

dance of stout cotton or thread. 1st. paste the strip of linen down the back and leave the book in the sun or near a fire—but not too near it—to dry, which it will do in half a day. 2ndly. Open the book and look for the place where the stitching is to be seen down the middle of the pages, or, in other words, for the middle of the sheets; if it be an 8vo. book it will be at every 16th page, if a 12mo. at every 24th page, and so on; it is a mere matter of semi-mechanical reckoning to know where each succeeding stitching is to be found . . . Next take the cotton and wind it between the pages where the stitching is, and over the back round and round, beginning with the first sheet until you have reached the last one. 3rdly. Lay the book on the table back upwards, daub it thoroughly with paste, put on the calico cover as neatly as you can, and set it to dry as before; when dry it is complete."[2]

[1]Francis Galton, *The Art of Travel* (1872): Or, Shifts and *Contrivances Available in Wild Countries* (Mechanicsburg, PA, Stackpole books, 1971)

[2]Ibid. p 329-30

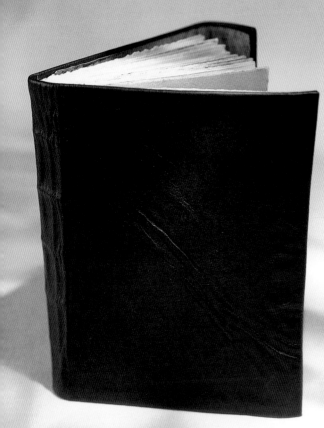

The Two-Hour leather-covered journal, sewn on cords

The Two-Hour Extremely Beautiful, Useful, and Sturdy Journal

For those of you who have actually enjoyed making your own journals by following the patterns above, this next—and final—journal is a modification of a traditional book form called a round-back book sewn on cords. It takes more time to make, but once you master it, it's possibly all the journal you will ever need or want. It's elegant, yet sturdy and rugged, and it feels good when you hold it in your hand. You can vary the size, shape, and materials to suit any needs you may have.

In order to sew a book on cords, you will need a piece of equipment called a sewing frame. While sewing frames are expensive and hard to find, you can make a very serviceable sewing frame from an old book in about 15 minutes for almost no cost (see the sidebar called Easy Sewing Frame on page 115).

TOOLS & MATERIALS

Text pages, whatever color, texture, weight, and size desired*

Cover material, preferably leather or canvas**

Sheet of paper to use for the end paper—it should be about the same weight as the text paper, and can actually be the same paper, or you can use decorative paper

Straight sewing needle with a large eye

Heavy cotton or linen thread, preferably bookbinders' thread—you can also use heavy sewing thread, embroidery floss, or dental floss

Metal ruler

Matt knife

Pushpin or awl

Piece of corrugated cardboard

Old telephone directory or thick magazine

PVA and a glue brush

Paste and a paste brush

Pencil

Black marker with a fine tip

Headband material or 1-inch-wide (2.5 cm) grosgrain ribbon (optional) sewing frame (See page 113)***

*First decide the size for your pages—and remember, not all pages need to be the same size. Buy enough paper to cut or tear into sheets that will be as high and twice as wide as the individual pages. For example, if you want the largest pages to be 6 x 9 inches (15.2 x 22.9 cm), cut the paper 12 x 9 inches (30.5 x 22.9 cm). Buy enough paper to make as many sheets as you want in the journal, realizing that you will be folding each sheet in half. Using at least 20 folded sheets of medium to heavyweight paper will make the spine fat enough to round nicely.

**The cover material needs to be about 1 inch (2.5 cm) higher than the text pages and around three times as wide. For a 6 x 9 (15.2 x 22.9 cm) page, you will need a piece of cover material approximately 18 x 10¼ inches (45.7 x 26 cm). The material can be a little less wide, but it's good to have enough to make a flap to protect the pages.

***Headband material is available through bookbinders' supply outlets or at some art supply stores.

Materials for making The Two-Hour Journal

INSTRUCTIONS

PREPARING THE PAGES

1 Cut or tear as much paper as needed for the text pages, then fold each piece of paper in half widthwise to form a folio. Nest the folios inside each other to form groups of folded pages known as *signatures*. The number of folios in a signature is determined by the weight of the paper you use. If the paper is relatively light, you can fit 6 or 7 sheets comfortably into one signature. For heavier paper, 3 or 4 may be the limit before the middle folios begin to protrude too far out from the front edge of the signature. Remember that pages don't all have to be the same size.

2 Cut or tear a piece of scrap paper that is 2 inches (5 cm) wide and the exact height of the signatures. This piece will become your pattern for punching the holes. Fold the pattern piece in half lengthwise, then unfold it, and fold it in half widthwise. Use a pencil to mark the center where the folds cross. Make another pencil mark in the vertical fold ½ inch (1.3 cm) up from the

bottom and ½ inch down from the top. Make two more marks, each ½ inch from the two end marks. Finally, make two marks midway between the center mark and the two marks in from the end marks, as shown in figure 1.

Figure 1

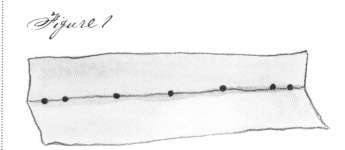

3 Open the telephone directory or magazine to a page near the middle. Follow the directions for hole punching in step 4 on page 101.

Note: After punching, there is no need to secure these signatures with paper clips.

SEWING THE TEXT BLOCK

4 To sew the text block, thread the needle with approximately 36 inches (91.5 cm) of thread. Use a single strand of thread for sewing, and do not tie a knot at the end. Lay the first signature on the sewing frame with its fold touching the strings, as shown in figure 2. Arrange each string to be next to one of the five central holes in the signature.

Note: The end holes are not associated with any strings. The horizontal string will hold the signature open while you sew. Tuck the pages of the signature that are closest to the strings *under* the horizontal string.

Figure 2

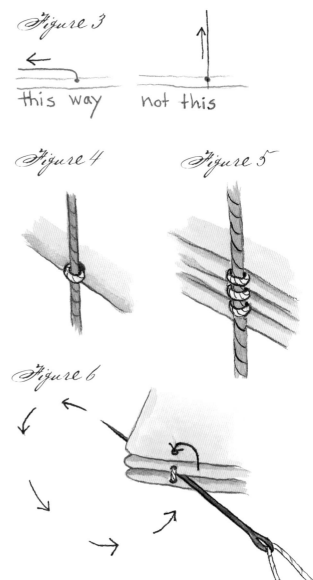

Figure 3

this way   not this

Figure 4   *Figure 5*

Figure 6

5 From the outside, insert the needle in either one of the end holes. Pull the thread, leaving a 3 or 4-inch (7.6 or 10.2 cm) tail. Next, from the inside, enter the next hole. The needle will come out of a hole near the first string, or cord. Pull the thread all the way until taut. Be careful to always tighten the thread by pulling parallel to the plane of the paper to avoid tearing, as shown in figure 3. Pass the needle over the cord and re-enter the same hole, pulling the thread so that it snugly covers the cord, as shown in figure 4.

6 Continue sewing this way until you have sewn around all five cords. Enter the last hole from the inside, and pull the thread taut. There is no cord next to the last hole.

7 Release the pages from the horizontal string by folding the signature, then lay the next signature on top of the first sewn signature. As you did for the first signature, open the second signature to its centerfold and tuck the pages under the horizontal string. Enter the end hole (the one that is nearest the needle) from the outside of the signature, and pull the thread taut to the inside. Sew this signature exactly as you did the first one. Bring the threads close together on the cords by using your fingers to gently press the signatures together, as shown in figure 5.

8 When you get to the end of the second signature, pull everything taut, and then tie the tail to the thread with a double knot. Do not cut the thread.

9 Close the second signature. Place the third one on top of it, open it, tuck the pages under the string, and sew this signature as you did the others. You should have three loops of thread over each cord when you finish sewing this signature. When you get to the end, you will need to join signature 3 to signature 2. To do this, make a loop stitch by slipping the needle behind the end stitch that is between the first and second signatures. Then enter the first hole of signature 3, as shown in figure 6.

10 Sew all the other signatures the same way, making a loop stitch at the end before joining the new signature.

Note: The loop stitch is done on the stitch between the two adjacent signatures (i.e., for signature 3, loop between signatures 2 and 1; for signature 4, loop between signatures 3 and 2; etc.). When you're finished sewing, tie a knot by slipping the needle under a stitch, making a few loops. Then cut the cords about 3 inches (7.6 cm) above and below the spine of the text block to remove the book from the frame.

MAKING THE COVER

11 To make the cover, cut the leather or canvas according to figure 7. If the leather is thin enough, allow for a ½-inch (1.3 cm) folded hem all the way around by adding the ½ inch to all edges. If the leather is too thick to fold, don't add the extra ½ inch to make a hem. You can do the same for canvas by either making a folded hem or leaving it unhemmed.

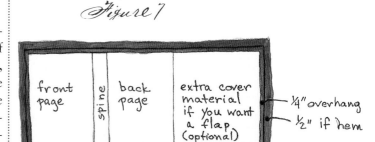

Figure 7

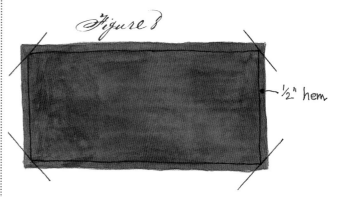

front page | spine | back page | extra cover material if you want a flap (optional)

— ¼" overhang
— ½" if hem

Figure 8

— ½" hem

12 If you're going to hem the leather or canvas, draw a fine line with a marker on the wrong side of the material ½ inch (1.3 cm) all around, and then cut a triangle from each corner, as shown in figure 8. Use PVA to adhere the hem. Be careful to wipe any drips or spills immediately. PVA stains leather and can't be removed once it dries.

ATTACHING THE COVER

13 To prepare the text block for gluing to the cover, first trim the cord ends to ½ inch (1.3 cm). Then hold the spine in one hand and grab the middle one-third of the pages, as shown in figure 9, and push in as indicated. This will slightly round the back or spine of the text block. When the spine is nicely rounded, close the text block, holding it as you do so as to maintain the rounding.

Figure 9

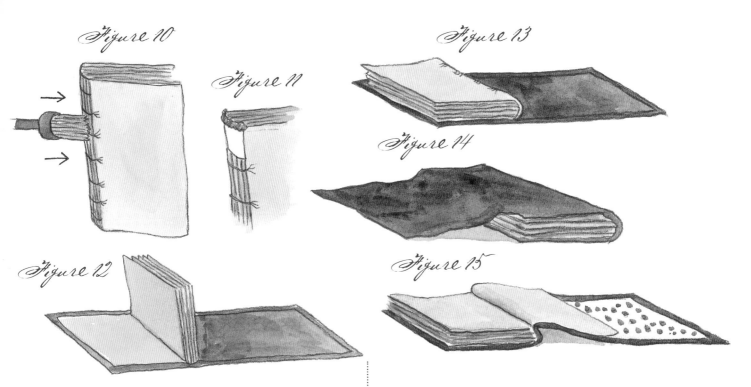

Figure 10

Figure 11

Figure 13

Figure 14

Figure 12

Figure 15

14 Apply PVA to the rounded spine to strengthen it. Using short pouncing motions, lightly push the glue brush repeatedly into the spine, as shown in figure 10. This allows you to apply the right amount of PVA—you want to get enough PVA between the signatures but don't want to apply too much or you will glue the pages together.

15 Carefully lay the glued text block on the edge of a table. Put a piece of scrap paper on top of the text block and then lay the closed telephone directory on top. This will gently compress the text block until it's dry.

16 If you're using a headband or ribbon, cut two pieces, each the width of the spine. Use PVA to glue them to the spine, as shown in figure 11.

17 To glue the text block to the cover, first put scrap paper between the first page and the rest of the text block to protect the pages. Then use a brush to apply paste over the entire page. Paste, unlike PVA that grabs more quickly and dries faster, will be easier to handle for this step since it allows you to reposition. However, you can use PVA if desired.

18 Remove the scrap paper. Lay the page with the pasted side down on the inside of the cover material, as shown in figure 12. Use your hands to rub and burnish the paper to adhere it to the cover material.

19 Put a clean piece of scrap paper on top of the page you've just pasted. Carefully close the text block, as shown in figure 13. Brush paste on the spine. Then place a piece of scrap paper under the top page as before to protect the other pages, and brush paste all over the top page. Remove the scrap paper. Wrap the cover material snugly around the text block. Be sure to pull the material tightly across the spine, as shown in figure 14.

20 Use your fingers to work the leather tight against the spine and the raised cords—you want the cords to show as bands across the back of the spine. Open the book slightly to check the position of the second piece of paper you've pasted in. If it's crooked—and only if you've used paste—peel back the cover and try again. Use your hands to rub and burnish both covers and the spine repeatedly until the leather adheres completely. Put the book aside to dry for several hours. If it's humid and you've used paste, drying can take as long as 24 hours. Note: Please be patient. If you open the book before it's completely dry, the spine will pull away from the cover and you must re-paste it.

21 If your cover has a flap and folded seams, you can give your journal a more finished look by applying an extra end paper. First, measure the length and width of the area on the inside covers where you will paste the end paper. Then cut or tear the end papers, coat the back of the paper with paste or PVA, and press it to the leather, as shown in figure 15.

Easy Sewing Frame

You won't have to worry about a big piece of equipment cluttering up your house with this sewing frame. It's made out of an old hardcover book—the pages are the platform of the sewing frame, and the covers hold the cords taut so you can sew on it. When you're not using this frame, you can just close it up and slide it back onto your bookshelf.

TOOLS & MATERIALS

Old hardcover book, at least 9 x 13 inches (22.9 x 33 cm)—bigger is better; old encyclopedias work well

Matt knife

7 small binder clips

1 very large binder clip

Ball of hemp, jute, or seine twine

INSTRUCTIONS

1 Using the matt knife, cut a window out of the front cover of the book. Leave about 1 inch (2.5 cm) at the top, bottom, and fore edge, and cut right along the crease at the spine. Open both covers and place the book on the edge of a table, as shown in figure 1.

2 To keep the top from slamming shut, attach the large binder and one small clip to bottom of the frame, as shown in figure 2.

3 Tie 5 strings to the top part of the frame. Use the small binder clips to attach them taut to the bottom of the back cover of the book, as shown in figure 3.

4 Tie a horizontal string about 3 inches (7.6 cm) from the large clip used for keeping the book open. Use a small clip to hold the string, making sure it's on the inside of the vertical cords and faces the pages of the book, as shown in figure 4.

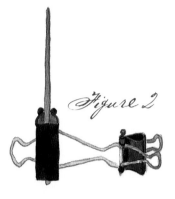

Figure 2

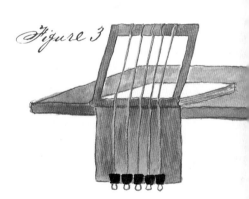

Figure 3

Figure 1

Figure 4

Customizing
a Blank Book

If you're not really interested in making your own journal, but the blank books you see for sale lack something, consider customizing a blank book. You can modify the pages to change the book form, as well as the cover. Following are some easy-to-make changes.

MODIFYING THE BOOK FORM

REMOVING PAGES

The secret to keeping a book from bulging open when you add elements to the pages is to equalize the fatness of the spine with the fatness of the fore edge of the book. There's nothing you can do to increase the fatness of the spine of a sewn or glued book. However, you can reduce the fatness of the fore edge so that any added elements would simply plump it back to its original size.

To do this, you will need to remove some pages. A rule of thumb is to remove one or two pages, depending on the thickness of the paper, for every page on which you intend to glue a collage element or photograph or any other added item. Keep in mind that this rule assumes that the added items are flat and are the approximate thickness of the removed page or pages.

To remove a page, first place a small, thin cutting mat under the page. Push the mat in toward the spine as far as it will easily go. Then use a ruler and matt knife to cut the page approximately ½ inch (1.3 cm) away from the spine edge. For a particular expressive reason, you might prefer to cut a wavy line or some irregular line instead of using a ruler. The resulting page stub can also become a design element. You can color it, draw on it, write on it, paint on it, etc.

ADDING AND CHANGING ELEMENTS

You might decide that you would like to add an envelope for collecting seeds, or some sheets of watercolor paper, grid paper, colored paper, tracing paper, or extremely beautiful wrapping paper from that small shop in the village you visited last weekend. To do this, begin by removing a page or two, depending on the thickness of the paper you will add, as directed in Removing Pages on page 116. Then, if you've removed one sheet, simply run a bead of PVA or roll a glue stick along the spine edge of the sheet you want to add, and press it to the front of the page stub. If you've cut off two pages, put adhesive on the front of the second stub, and lay the additional element onto it. Then run another bead of adhesive along the back of the first page stub and press it on top of the spine edge of the add-on element.

LAMINATING PAGES

You can laminate, or completely adhere, one page on top of another page in the book. If the paper that you want to laminate is on the heavy or moderately heavy side, you'll need to remove the page that comes before the page you wish to laminate to accommodate the different weight paper. Depending on the thickness, you may need to remove the page after as well. Then simply cut the element you want to laminate to the size of the page to which it will be laminated, minus a vertical strip along the spine edge that is the same size as the page stub left from removing the preceding page.

Spread adhesive over the back of the element to be laminated (see Adhesives on page 31 to determine the best adhesive for the job). Line up the element with the fore edge of the base page, and press the pages together. Slip pieces of wax paper into the book on top and below the laminated page, and close the book to press the pages while they dry.

If the book is going to have different sections that you'll want to locate quickly, consider laminating a tabbed divider page at the beginning of each section. Follow the directions for laminating a page, but cut the page to add a tab at the top or fore edge side, making the tab extend ¼ inch (6 mm) or so beyond the pages of the book.

PIGGYBACKS

A piggyback is a small journal that rides along inside the main journal and can be taken out on its own when you don't feel like carrying the big journal. First, you can make a pocket for the piggyback to ride in. You can do this by trimming a page to become the front of the envelope. Then glue or stitch along the top and bottom edges of two pages, as shown in figure 1. You'll need to remove two or three pages to accommodate the thickness of the piggyback. Make a single-signature pamphlet as described on page 100, slip it into the pocket, and away you go.

Another kind of piggyback is an accordion. Make a pocket as described above. Fold a long, narrow sheet of paper back and forth several times to form a small accordion book. Remove the next few pages to accommodate the thickness of the accordion, and slip the accordion into the pocket. This is a particularly useful piggyback for a map.

Figure 1

Modifying the Cover

ENCRUSTATION

A hard-cover book can be completely transformed by a process called encrustation that was developed by book artist Timothy Ely. The effects that you can achieve by means of this process are limited only by your imagination.

TOOLS & MATERIALS

Acrylic matte medium

Quart (.95 L) jar

Thickener or texturizing material such as whiting powder or talc for a smooth texture, sand for a rougher texture, and small seashells, pebbles, or seeds for a coarse texture

Spoon

Masking tape

Small squares of cardboard, mat board, or old credit cards

Dinner knife, palette knife, or putty knife

Materials for embedding, such as small scraps of cardboard and leather, twigs, mica, shells, cloth

Liquid acrylic paints

INSTRUCTIONS

1 Pour about 1 inch (2.5 cm) of matte medium into the jar. Add whiting, talc, sand, or other thickener to make a thick paste. Stir until completely mixed.

2 If the book has a spine that you don't want to encrust, cover it with masking tape before proceeding. If you want a design that is raised above the surface of the book, glue on pieces of cardboard, mat board, or old credit cards to form these relief areas.

3 Trowel the encrusting material onto one cover of the book, spreading it as you go. Cover the entire surface except for any areas that are masked off.

Gwen Diehn, *South Haven Journal*, 2003. 6 x 9 inches (15.2 x 22.9 cm). Leather-covered spine, book board encrusted with sand and beach glass

If you want a particularly thick encrustation and you don't want it to crack, it's better to do it in several layers, letting each layer dry completely before going on to each subsequent one.

4 Embed pieces of mica, cloth, rocks, beads, etc. by pushing or pressing them into the encrustation.

5 Let the encrustation dry. This may take several hours, depending on the humidity and the thickness of the encrustation.

6 Once the surface is completely dry, it can be sanded, carved into with carving tools, or scored with nails or a knife. Paint the encrustation with liquid acrylics and polish it with shoe polish. Carefully peel off any masking tape.

An encrusted cover in process

7 A finish coat of paste wax can protect as well as add luster.

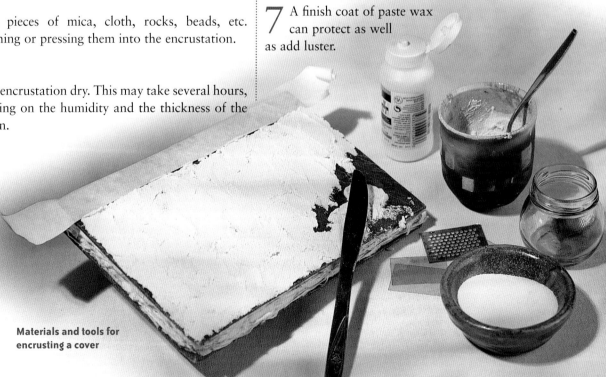

Materials and tools for encrusting a cover

COLLAGE

Either hard or softcovers can be changed by collage.

TOOLS AND MATERIALS

Old newspapers to put under work

PVA

Glue brush

Heavyweight acrylic mediums, such as gel medium, garnet gel, and absorbent ground

Polymer varnish—satin, flat, or gloss finish

1-inch (2.5 cm) soft, flat paintbrush

Materials to collage, such as paper, cloth, thin leather, etc.

INSTRUCTIONS

1 Brush PVA over the backs of the items to be collaged. Press collage items into place on the hard or soft-cover. You can use gel mediums and absorbent ground to build up areas that you can carve, paint, and collage over.

2 After the collage is dry, add any drawing or writing as desired.

3 Repeat for the other cover.

4 When the entire book is dry, varnish with two coats of polymer varnish.

Gwen Diehn, *Untitled Journal*. 6 x 9 inches (15.2 x 22.9 cm). Journal covered with collage of pieces of old drawings and monotypes then covered with glossy polymer varnish.

Juliana Coles, *In Transition: Hold Fast*, 2000-2001. 10 x 8³/₄ x 1¹/₂ inches (25.4 x 22.2 x 3.8 cm). Hardbound journal, watercolor paper, watercolor crayon, china marker, craft acrylics, pen and ink, rubber stamp letters; collaged. Photo by Pat Berrett

Stenciling letters onto a cover

LETTERING

Add a title to any book by carefully lettering with a stencil and ink or paint that is compatible with the surface. If the surface is very shiny or rough, follow the directions below for making a label.

TOOLS & MATERIALS

Matt knife

Ruler

PVA

Glue brush

Paper label with lettering printed on it

INSTRUCTIONS

1 With the ruler and matt knife, carefully trace a shallow cut around the outside of the label into the cover, just deep enough to penetrate the outer layers of the cover material.

2 Peel the outer layers of cover material up from inside the cut lines.

3 Paint the paper label with PVA and press it into place in the peeled-off area.

4 Varnish the paper label with matt finish polymer varnish.

DRAWING

If the book has a smooth cover, draw and paint directly on it with acrylics.

Julie Wagner, *Chronicle of Sleepless Nights*, 2002. $9^1/_8$ x $8^7/_8$ x $^3/_4$ inches (23.2 x 22.5 x 1.9 cm). Stab-bound journal, handmade Japanese paper, handmade Nepalese paper, ink, oil transfer drawings. Photo by Dan Morse

ALTERING A BOOK

An alternative to using a new blank book or to making a book yourself is to use an existing book as the basis of your journal. Much has been written on the subject of altering books, and this will be only a brief introduction. Begin by finding a book that means something to you. It might be a book from your childhood, or a book on a subject that continues to interest you. It might be a book that you simply like for its size, shape, weight of paper, and cover.

The first step in reclaiming this book is to prepare the pages to receive your work. If the paper is old and somewhat fragile, a coat of wheat paste sizing will help to stabilize them a little. Make a batch of wheat paste following directions on page 33. Place a piece of blotter paper under the page, and brush the paste onto the page. You'll need to allow each page to dry before working on it or turning to the next page. A hair dryer can speed up the process.

Another way to prepare a page is to brush it with slightly thinned absorbent ground or with acrylic gesso (see Grounds, page 38). Yet another way to block out the parts of the page that you want to write or draw on is to paint over it with gouache (see Gouache, page 24).

Remember that if the pages are made of thin paper, they will wrinkle and cockle when you apply wet media to them. You can prepare very thin pages by using light colored or white water-soluble crayons, but not wetting them. And of course pages can be covered at least partially with collage. Use a glue stick if the paper is on the thin side.

Using an Old Book Cover

If you're mainly interested in putting new pages or a text block into an altered book, a trip to a used bookstore can provide a fine journal cover. After making The Thirty-Minute Multi-Pamphlet Journal on page 106, you can slip the pages into a cover of your choice for a unique and interesting journal.

TOOLS & MATERIALS

Text block made by following instructions for the Thirty-Minute Pamphlet*

Old book

*The page size of the new text block should be the same as the pages you are removing from the old book.

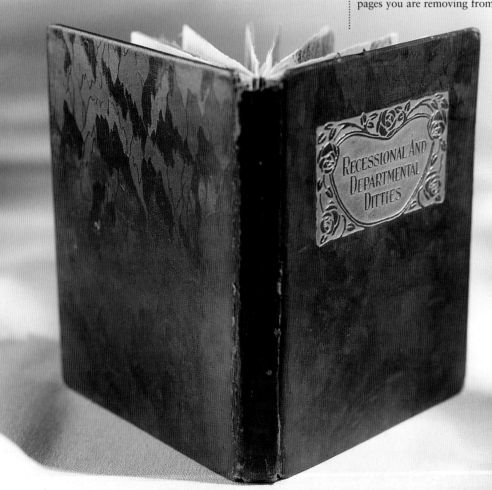

INSTRUCTIONS

1 Using a matt knife, carefully cut the old text block from its cover by cutting the end papers in the joint or fold of the inside covers. Take care to cut through the paper only and not the book's covering material.

2 Place scrap paper between the first and second sheet of the new text block to protect them. Brush paste all over the outside sheet of the text block. Lay the pasted page over the inside of the front cover, as shown in figure 1 and burnish thoroughly.

3 Lay a sheet of scrap paper between the newly pasted end paper and the text block. Close the book with the newly pasted side down.

4 Repeat steps 2 and 3 on the other side. Note: that the spine of the text block is not glued to the spine board of the cover. If you want to further persue making your own journal you'll find a bibliography for "not-so-reluctant" book binders on page 127.

Kelcey Loomer, *Untitled Journal Page*, 2001. 11 x 8¹/₄ inches (27.9 x 21 cm)
Bound journal, acrylic paint, ink, pen, excerpt from a phone message. Photo by artist

Afterword

Once I started making my own journals a number of years ago, I actually found myself enjoying the process. Since they were purely personal and utilitarian books, not museum pieces or even structures to turn into artists' books or gifts for friends, I could relax and chalk up to experience the inevitable early-on bad choices that led to awkward construction. Relaxing meant that I got better at the craft more quickly than if I had been under pressure to make a beautiful book every time. Pretty soon I had found a form or two that I liked very much as well as a range of papers that suited my way of working.

I began to enjoy the process of preparing for a special project or a trip away from home by making a journal in anticipation of the event. I actually started cutting and folding pages and making the covers of travel journals before I left home, and then sewing the books en route. The next step was to bring along a few folded pieces of paper, a needle and thread and a push pin and paper clip and make the whole journal at the beach or at night in my hotel room, using additional materials gathered on site—special papers, maps, ephemera, and a few locally obtained art supplies.

Of course there have been times when I actually did stumble upon a ready-made journal that was exactly what I wanted at that particular time. I dearly love my small quadrille paper Junior Sum Copy Book from a small grocery store in County Clare. And the tiny leather-covered Italian journal given to me by one of my sons became a prototype for several journals, simply because I loved using the original so much. One of my all-time favorite journals is a facsimile of one of Van Gogh's sketchbooks that my husband bought for me at the bookstore of the Metropolitan Museum of Art a number of years ago.

But these are exceptions. The majority of my journals are homemade. And though they may lack a certain level of perfection in craftsmanship, their often experimental forms—in the exact size and shape I need and with their perfect choice of paper—still please me very much and continue to serve me well. I wish you the same pleasure with your journals, both in the making and in the keeping of them.

Acknowlegments

Writing this book has felt like a long conversation with many people over the past year. It has been a collaborative effort in many ways. Gratitude, then, to my students at Warren Wilson College as well as in the workshops I've taught this year and last—yours are the questions and ideas and enthusiasm that has driven the project. Thanks also to the many journal keepers on several internet lists for artists journals and especially on Danny Gregory's Everyday Matters list: your questions and constant search for ideas and information convinced me that there might be a place in the growing body of journal-keeping literature for yet another book on the subject.

Many thanks to friends and colleagues for ideas, information, and insights, especially Ann Turkle, Noah Saterstrom, Dusty Benedict, Bette Bates, Jane Dalton, Sandy Webster, Edie Greene, and Coral Jensen. Special thanks to the women in Park Slope who fed me wonderful breakfasts and traded ideas when I was in Brooklyn during the year—especially Faith, Dana, and Zoe. Thanks to Aleia Woolsey for help with photography.

I would get nowhere fast without the love and support of my family, Phil, Michael, David, Erik, Andi, Kristie, Kerstin, and Jacob, Tallis, Luca, and Maya. They not only provided tangible help (Michael even took dictation over the phone one night when I felt like I could not type another word, and emailed me the manuscript a few minutes later) but also their ideas and responses. Kerstin and Jacob loaned me their own journals for use in the book.

Special thanks to those at Lark Books including my smart and sensitive editor at Lark, Jane LaFerla, always the book's champion; to art director Susan McBride for an elegant design; and to associate editor Susan Keiffer for tracking down all the permissions and for research assistance.

A NOTE ABOUT SUPPLIERS

Usually, the supplies you need for making the projects in Lark books can be found at your local craft supply store, discount mart, home improvement center, or retail shop relevant to the topic of the book. Occasionally, however, you may need to buy materials or tools from specialty suppliers. In order to provide you with the most up-to-date information, we have created a list of suppliers on our website, which we update on a regular basis. Visit us at www.larkbooks.com, click on "Craft Supply Sources," and then click on the relevant topic. You will find numerous companies listed with their web address and/or mailing address and phone number.

Bibliography

Bookbinding for Book Artists by Keith Smith; Keith a Smith Books; 1998; ISBN 0963768255

Books, Boxes & Portfolios: Binding, Construct and Design, Step by Step by Franz Zeier; McGraw-Hill Professional; 1990 ISBN 0830634835

Cover to Cover: Creative Techniques for Making Beautiful Books, Journals & Albums by Shereen LaPlantz; Sterling Publishers; 1998 ISBN 0937274879

Contributing Artists

Pamela Averick 54
Sarah A. Bourne 19, 40, 70, 71, 73
Traci Bunkers 79, 97
Justin S. Catalini 85
Tara Chickey 39
Juliana Coles 41, 97, 120
Betsy Couzins, 96
Jane Dalton 57, 82, 98
Wendy Hale Davis 36
Jacob Diehn 95
Clare Duplace 69, 87
Jeanne G. Germani 50
Scott Gordon 76
Edie Greene 53, 87
Megan Gulledge 88
Charlotte Hedlund 56, 83
Aude Iung-Lancrey 96
Dana Fox Jenkins 78
Rebecca Johnson 32-33, 84
Eric Larson 46
Kristin A. Livelsberger 77
Kelcey Loomer 28, 29, 42, 49, 60, 64, 75, 97, 124
Val Lucas 60
Amber Maloy 21
Faith McLellan 62, 90
Miriam McNamara 94
Mary Ann Moss 73
Joseph A. Osina 48
Andrea A. Peterson 37, 63
Nancy Pobanz 92
Victoria Rabinowe 65
Judy Rinks 90
Matt Rogers 22, 88
Janet Scholl 57
Ivy Smith 8, 86
Billie Jean Theide 45
Ann Turkle 52, 66, 67
Kerstin Vogdes 12, 13, 53, 54, 59
Julie Wagner 17, 65, 121
Sandy Webster 46

Index